GOD
KNOWS

Wisdom for Everyday Living

PASTOR CHARLES L. ORR

Edited by:

ANNE COOPER READY

WESTBOW
PRESS®
A DIVISION OF THOMAS NELSON
& ZONDERVAN

WestBow Press books may be ordered through booksellers or by contacting:

WestBow Press
A Division of Thomas Nelson & Zondervan
1663 Liberty Drive
Bloomington, IN 47403
www.westbowpress.com
1 (866) 928-1240

Because of the dynamic nature of the Internet, any web addresses or links contained in this book may have changed since publication and may no longer be valid. The views expressed in this work are solely those of the author and do not necessarily reflect the views of the publisher, and the publisher hereby disclaims any responsibility for them.

ISBN: 978-1-9736-3272-6 (sc)
ISBN: 978-1-9736-3271-9 (hc)
ISBN: 978-1-9736-3273-3 (e)

Library of Congress Control Number: 2018907708

Print information available on the last page.

WestBow Press rev. date: 10/08/2018

For Claire and David, with whom we've been blessed

CONTENTS

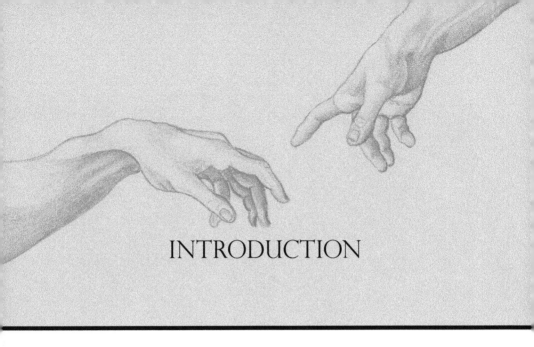

INTRODUCTION

How often we look to Heaven with a shake of the head and say, "God knows!" It means we don't know, but He does.

And, as Pastor Charles explains, God's undying love will strengthen and sustain us though our journeys. And encourages us to share His love with others.

What makes this book particularly unique are Pastor Charles' insights illuminated by the quotes of influential people representing an array of philosophies. He includes relevant Bible verses, scenes from movies and plays and stanzas from beloved poems and favorite songs.

On these pages, Pastor Charles explores the mysteries and challenges of life in new and contemporary ways. He takes a common sense approach to such issues as: Uncertainty & Faith, Feeling Guilty, The Blessings of Loneliness, Recovering Self-Worth, When There's Nothing You Can Do, Loving & Hurting, Leaving Home and Who Am I?

Let *GOD KNOWS: Wisdom for Everyday Living* be as daily bread, a resource of God's love. A gift for yourself and others.

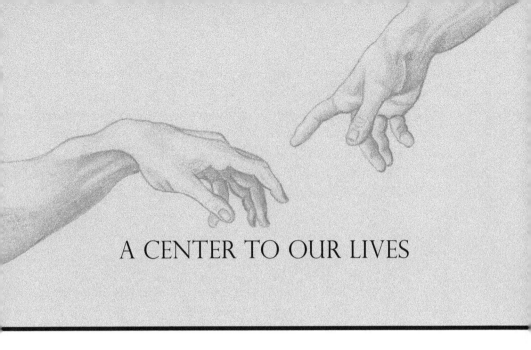

A CENTER TO OUR LIVES

Albert Camus – the great French writer who caught the contradictions and loneliness of contemporary life – reintroduced to modern man an ancient Greek myth, the myth of Sisyphus.

Sisyphus was like a modern man or woman. He had come of age. He scorned the gods, hated death, and was passionately attached to life.

For his audacity and passions, the gods placed him in eternal punishment and assigned him one specific task. He was compelled to push a huge rock up a mountainside.

And when he got the rock to the top, it would come crashing down again. And Sisyphus had to start all over.

Now we have to confess that Camus is right – at least partly.

Life seems that way at times. You give it all you've got and begin to think maybe that's enough, and then it comes rolling back on you. You struggle to overcome a deficiency, in self–esteem, for example. And suddenly, your heroic efforts are interrupted by someone who puts you down – hard. To find hope in this world – and keep it – seems as futile as Sisyphus' task.

Yet, the Apostle Paul wrote that the early Christians did not lose heart. They believed that the outward man does indeed suffer wear and tear, but everyday the inward man receives fresh strength.

Now, how do we square this with our experience? How do we make sense of it if we indeed are all Sisyphuses, pushing our dreadful rock until one day it finally rolls back and crushes us?

Paul faced the absurdities and contradictions of life, too – the ragged edges, the falling rocks are all there in his biography. He was put down because of a weak body and inelegant speech, plagued by some sort of illness, which never remitted. He was stoned, beaten, shipwrecked, accused. He suffered anxiety and stress over the frail little churches he had founded here and there.

Once, the early Christians were so utterly, unbearably crushed that they despaired of life itself.

Yet, they never collapsed. Why?

Because in faith, Paul trusted not in his own power, but the power of God. In faith, he grasped the presence of God, even in the midst of agonies, working out His purposes of love and justice.

Faith became a key to see something new. Paul wrote that to believe in God is to believe that there is more to experience than the obvious.

Now, for 21st Century people, that's hard to hear. We live in a world filled with obvious disasters and threats. Some of us can still remember a global war, preceded by terrible depression, assassinations of our leaders, attacks in our country and on innocent children. We've witnessed great international blunders and tragedies; we seem to reel from one domestic crisis to another.

And the sense of frustration of the larger world matches the absurdities of our own personal world, too.

But the Biblical writers bid us to look deeper and realize that things are not always what they seem.

Imagine a scenario in which the powers of evil should have full rein.

- Suppose wickedness, injustice, corruption, stupidity and violence should run amuck and smother righteousness.
- Suppose a saint should appear in whom all that is affirming, all that is holy love was perfectly reflected here on earth.
- Suppose a day would come when the sky darkens and the earth quakes and this good man dies without a flicker of comfort from Heaven or earth.

What then? Could we have any hope? But it happened, you know. All this did happen. The Church is here today to remind us that it happened.

The cross – a strange symbol of evil and execution – became transmuted into the most piercing symbol of love the world can ever know – because God is in the midst of it.

That's what Paul knew. That's why he could write that the early Christians did not lose heart. To believe in the One who came in Jesus Christ is to believe that there is more to experience than the obvious.

According to Paul, to believe in Him who overcomes the final negation of human existence is to believe in the future. Paul wrote that we must look not at the visible things, but at the invisible. The visible things are transitory, it is the invisible things that are really permanent.

Christian faith is not simple-minded, a chirpy belief that everything will get better in every way. Rather, it is the determined conviction that no matter how bad things get, God is yet working for good. That even from man's evil, God can bring good.

This faith is challenged on many, many fronts. Nowhere is the belief more critical than in the arena of human suffering and tragedy, where many despair of belief.

But on the other hand, living without faith in God leaves only ourselves on which to anchor hope. If we are Sisyphus, rolling a rock up the mountain, knowing that sooner or later, it will roll back on us again, how can we have hope?

The old legend speaks some truth about us.

But then? Then, all the more need for an Other. A Greater than man, a meaning beyond man's meaningless rock rolling; a hidden reality greater than fateful plodding and pushing. One who can shoulder the load when it is simply too much for us.

The hope we have in God – the One whom we meet in the crucified and risen Christ – gives a center to life that we do not otherwise have. Is this not what we need now? A Center to our lives, something, which helps us give order and reason and meaning and momentum. Without it, don't we all become outliers.

Life with God – life with centeredness – enables us to keep on keeping on – living in the awareness of the unseen, yet permanent possibilities, which lie ahead.

Christ is risen; Christ is risen, indeed. And we are all included. There is hope.

Prayer: Dear Lord, let me never forget that all things work together for good, to them that love God and are called according to His purposes.

Amen

A HAPPENING OF GRACE

Tucked away in the Old Testament, in the Book of Kings, is a story of unusual faith found in an unlikely place.

Not unlike recent times in America, Israel had been experiencing a prolonged drought – but the dry and parched land was not nearly so barren as the hearts of faithless people. The light of faith in the God of the Covenant – of Abraham and Moses – seemed almost totally extinguished by King Ahab and his idolatrous wife, Jezebel.

But in those years of flickering faith and harsh conditions, the light refused to be snuffed out.

North of Israel – in Gentile territory – at a little nowhere village called Zarephath, there lived a widow. She had but one meager meal between herself and starvation. She gathered firewood to prepare the meal so that she and her son could eat before they die. There was nothing left – and no hope for anything at all.

Surely we, who look out upon the starving people of our world today, get the picture.

But Elijah, the prophet, implored her as she prepared for the last meal, to feed him first. And promised that the God of Israel would provide that the jar of meal would not be spent. And the cruse of oil would not fail until the day that the Lord sent rain upon the earth.

The small loaf that would have kept death at bay for a few more days was now given away. All that stood between her and death was God. She trusted Him.

This ancient story was to be recalled years later in the notorious Nazi camp at Ravensbrück, where Corrie Ten Boom and her sister, Betsie had been shipped after they were discovered hiding Jews in their home. Somehow, Corrie had managed to procure a small bottle of liquid vitamins. She had tried to hoard it for her sister who was growing so weak, but there were others who were also in desperate need of the precious vitamins.

Listen to Corrie Ten Boom's words: "And still, every time I tilted the little bottle, a drop appeared at the tip of the glass stopper. It just couldn't be. I held it up to the light trying to see how much was left, but the dark brown glass was too thick to see through."

"'There was a woman in the Bible,' Betsie said, 'whose oil jar was never empty'. She turned to it in the Book of Kings, the story of the poor widow of Zarephath, who gave Elijah a room in her home. And the jar of meal wasted not, neither did the cruse of oil fail, according to the word of Jehovah, which he spoke by Elijah.

"Well, but, wonderful things happened all through the Bible. It was one thing to believe that such things were possible thousands of years ago, another to have it happen now, to us, this very day. And yet it happened, this day, and the next, and the next, until an awed little group of spectators stood around watching the drops fall onto the daily rations of bread.

"Many nights, I lay awake in the shower of straw dust from the mattress above, trying to fathom the marvel of supply lavished upon us. 'Maybe,' I whispered to Betsie, 'only a molecule or two really gets through that little pinhole – and then in the air it expands!'

"I heard her soft laughter in the dark: 'don't try too hard to explain it, Corrie. Just accept is as a surprise from a Father who loves you.'

"Later, when one of the women in the barracks managed to steal a supply of vitamin tablets and a large jar of yeast, then – strangely – the small bottle of liquid vitamins failed to produce another drop."

Thus, the ancient story resonates amidst the horrors of the 20th Century.

In the New Testament, Mark closes his record of the public ministry of Jesus, both appropriately and prophetically with the story of another poor widow who in Jesus' words, gave all that she had.

Now, it seems to me that we who encounter these stories, must beware of the temptation to somehow idealize the poverty of the poor. There is nothing virtuous about poverty. All of us are human, and the poor can be as infected with the venom of fear and destructive impulses as can the rapacious rich.

What needs to be borne in mind is that the poor widow – like the blind beggar, like the little child – is the biblical image for emptiness before God.

To be empty means to have the capacity to be filled. And that means receiving something – not giving and not doing, but receiving. And here we encounter a paradox: having been rid of everything, having stood empty and poor without claim before God, one is strangely able to receive everything – even one's own life as a gift.

All of us have experienced this in our own lives, praying on some occasion when we hit bottom. Praying a prayer of renunciation, of emptiness, of resources and need. And we were filled. This mystery means something for all. For each of us has to deal with ourselves – and with others -- which means we deal somehow always with the problem of validating our own existence.

And it is always difficult to put aside those mechanisms of self-justification, which we have refined over our lifetimes. And simply let go, simply allow ourselves to stand in the sheer emptiness of our humanity. And receive that which we in no way can claim to have earned or inherited.

Now this is, admittedly, difficult to grasp. For it has to do with the gospel, with the gift God gives. And it is so foreign to the usual flow of transactions in this world that we keep taking Christianity and squeezing it through another grid. So that it comes out – subtly or blatantly -- that we must earn God's grace. If, by nothing more, than the strength of our faith.

We do have to <u>do</u> something – or <u>refrain</u> from doing something, we're told – in order to find any ultimate validation for our existence.

Thus, all too often, the Church has made God into a great celestial nag, who says: "Read this book or that, go to church regularly and to all its special services, pray so many times a day, tutor the children, and befriend patients in the hospitals. And if you do all these good works, then I will reward you with the assurance you have earned your salvation."

And this formula is not limited to the Church; the para-religious therapies that abound offer people some technique, some system that promises to relieve the anxiety of being human. If one will only subscribe, do, fold, support; one will be validated.

How many people do you know who rush from this system to that system looking vainly for that which neither their money nor anything else can buy?

The good news is that for which we search is already given to us in the mysterious and unconditional love of God. Glimpsed essentially in the life, death and resurrection of One who commends a poor widow who gives all that she has.

How is this good news heard? Perhaps, I think best from other caring people; perhaps in a book or on a stage or screen, maybe even in a sermon. But hear it, a person must. For wholeness (salvation) involves being able to accept ourselves as we really are. And the only force that allows that is love – which is always a gift.

Prayer: Dear Lord, give me the courage to accept myself as empty before you and in need of being filled by your love.

Amen

ALONE AT LAST

Alone at last! How many times have you ever longed to say those words, to relish the occasions that they anticipate?

The moment, for instance, when the last job for the day is done, when the children are in bed. And the book, which you just couldn't put down – but had to – is beckoning.

Then, at last, you can be with your book.

Or, alone at last – when the guests have gone, the party's over, the fire is burning low, the stereo's playing soft music and you're alone with someone you love.

Alone at last. Those kinds of moments of aloneness are welcome and necessary oases in our journeys through life. We all need them. We all cherish them.

But there are other moments of aloneness, which are not so welcome. Indeed, which we may dread. Moments when, for instance, we wait alone in some clinic's cubicle, or outside a courtroom, for the results of a test or for someone's judgment, which will change our lives forever.

It is then that we confront another kind of aloneness. An inevitable aloneness, which is, we know at some deep level, only a kind of foretaste for that final aloneness that will come to each of us in the moment of our dying. When, in the final sense of those words, we must say: "I'm alone at last."

Now, we are not made in our humanity to welcome death, nor should we, I believe, dwell inordinately upon it. Nonetheless, there is a need to know that being totally alone in that sense is partly – if only the final part – of our human experience. And, therefore, it does have some fundamental value to us, which needs to be appreciated and understood.

Ruell Howe, a wise Christian teacher and counselor, reminds us that, "You can't be human alone."

And that is true. But the other side of that truth is that you can't be fully human if you are not able to appreciate the full dimension of individuality. At the root of our humanity is that each one of us is unique. And it is here that our finitude – our awareness of existential aloneness in these experiences – is a foretaste of death. It underscores our sense of uniqueness, that sense of separation from everything and everyone else, that sense of distinction from all other people and places and events.

Alone at last. This is, indeed, the end-point of our life's journey. But it is also, in some strange way, the goal of our inward journey, as well. That secret journey where we know for certain our uniqueness -- and are able to say with a sense of peace – I am alone at last.

This is never an easy journey, this inward journey. But it is an utterly fascinating human one. We all must take it if we are to be human, if we are to be ourselves.

And in this journey, there are moments when we sort out our experiences and sum up what meaning we can discern and trace in our lives.

How do I begin to sort out, how do I begin to try to sum up the elusive self who is somehow me?

There is never a tidy blueprint. Perhaps, the first step though, is to recognize that we do have an inward and an outward self, a private and a public persona.

The outward self is the self we present to the world. And this self is necessary for our identity and for our survival. Just as the animal needs camouflage, so we need our outward self to protect our inward self.

Having recognized that we do possess this sort of double life, we then must become as deeply aware as possible of the inwardness of ourselves. For the outwardness of our lives does have a way of looking after itself; it is the inside, the inward journey, which requires more attention.

In Graham Greene's great modern classic, *The Power and The Glory,* our hero (or non-hero) is a seedy, alcoholic Catholic priest. After months as a fugitive, he is finally caught by the revolutionary Mexican government and condemned to be shot.

On the evening before his execution, he sits in his cell with a flask of brandy to keep his courage up and thinks back over what seems to him the dingy failure of his life.

"Tears poured down his face," Greene writes. "He was not at that moment afraid of damnation – even the fear of pain was in the background. He felt only an immense disappointment because he had to go to God empty-handed, with nothing accomplished at all.

"It seemed to him at that moment that it would have been quite easy to have been a saint. He would only have needed a little self-restraint and a little courage. He felt like someone who had missed happiness by seconds at an appointed place. He knew now that at the end, there was only one thing that counted – to be a saint."

To know Christ – that was the end of his inward journey. To live and die as a recipient of grace – that is as one who is given a gift and the ability to receive that gift. The gift of knowledge that I am loved deeply and accepted permanently as I really am.

When this gift is received – if only tenuously, if only in part – then somehow that frantic struggle to validate one's own existence through the careful cultivation of the external, outward life begins to fade away.

Yes -- your brains, your brawn, your skill, your beauty, your charm, your fame and fortune – all of these may be wonderful aspects of your life. But they are not the total sum of your life. And your life is not secured by attachment to any one of them.

There is something more to your life. Something, which lies deep inside, which hungers and thirsts for something permanent.

Security and a sense of significance ultimately cannot come from outside. It cannot come from conformity to images of power and success dictated by society – no matter how altruistic they may be.

The good news is that at the moment we begin to glimpse our need, the gift is at hand. There is something deep, which is rooted in all of us – which breaks through – sometimes in the most unlikely places.

Holocaust survivor, Viktor Frankl wrote in *A Man's Search For Meaning* of the horror of Nazi concentration camps, the brutality and death ...

"there in the cramped and smelly hut, these men are separated from loved ones and their futures and were aware that they would likely soon be dead."

He writes of trying to help them gain perspective by showing how, even then, their situation was not the most terrible they could imagine. He spoke of the future and their awareness of the small chance for survival. He spoke also of the past and its joys. He continued, "then I spoke of the many opportunities of giving life a meaning. I told my comrades (who lay motionless, although occasionally a sigh could be heard) that human life, under any circumstances, never ceases to have a meaning. The infinite meaning of life includes suffering and dying, privation and death. I asked the poor creatures (who listened to me attentively in the darkness of the hut) to face up to the seriousness of our position. They must not lose hope. But must keep their courage in the certainty that the hopelessness of our struggle did not detract from its dignity and meaning." His efforts were rewarded by the tears of gratitude in the eyes of those who came to offer him thanks.

There is about us all an irreducible uniqueness – which we affirm beyond all ideologies. We are infinitely precious because we have on us the signature of the Creator. Sealed if you will, by the blood of Christ. And that binds us in our very uniqueness – and this bears witness to the meaning of all human life.

The knowledge of the divine in us, of the Christ who comes to dwell in us, is the prize at the end of the journey inward.

Prayer: Dear Lord, let me take my inward journey with Thee.

Amen

AN ONGOING DRAMA

Have you ever experienced yourself as somehow more than one person – as if you were living in the midst of many selves?

It is an assertion of one direction of psychological thinking that none of us are single persons, having only one personality and one way of life. We are extraordinarily complex. We are, in sum, many people.

"I am large," cried Walt Whitman, American poet and humanist, "I contain multitudes."

Psychiatrist and founder of analytical psychology, Carl Jung called these complexes "the little people." In a lecture several years ago, James Hillman, then Director of the Jungian Institute in Zurich, confessed: "I give an order to myself and a whole platoon marches in the wrong direction."

People laughed nervously – for something very revealing had been said.

In Luke's Gospel, the parable of the Rich Man and Lazarus contains, if not a whole platoon of characters, at least several of Jung's "little people." And in it, we can discover something about ourselves. First, as the Rich Man, Dives; then as the Poor Man, Lazarus and; finally, as one of the Five Brothers who wait for a signal from God.

Jesus is saying something to each of these little people within us … the parable is a drama in two acts.

In Act I, we encounter the rich man, Dives – richly clothed and fed.

13

Outside his gate lies Lazarus – too weak from hunger to drive off the scavenger dogs that lick his sores.

The indictment against Dives is <u>not</u> because he is rich – but because he is indifferent. He chooses to avoid the Lazaruses of this world. He doesn't want to confront the human misery, human death or the dark contingencies and inequities of existence that Lazarus represents.

So Dives avoids him. And therefore he avoids something else, too. Some part of himself and that Other to whom he is ultimately accountable for his soul, God.

Rich Dives treats miserable Lazarus as if the poor man doesn't exist – the all-too-familiar story of the invisible poor among us.

But, my friend, who among us is not rich? If not in money, then at least in experience. And in the capacity to give of ourselves, to some poor Lazarus who happens to be lying at our own doorstep. Some Lazarus, who may be starving for a sign of affirmation; a hunger for understanding; a word of hope, that somehow she or he is not alien to the human condition.

And aren't these gifts, which to some extent, each of us possesses? Unless they are used, are we not then Dives, locked away from others? And ultimately an important part of ourselves, which needs to relate and give?

Next, we encounter Lazarus – the poor man, whose name incidentally means in Hebrew "one whom God helps." Now the fact is, that apart from God, nobody pays attention to him.

Yet, in the Bible, poverty means not only the lack of money. It also means coming to the realization that human life is filled with deep and profound needs. "Deep calleth unto deep," quotes the psalmist, in Psalms 42:17, meaning discovering a deeper relationship with God.

We are so constituted that none of us is meant to go it alone through life. That ultimately we cannot be fulfilled, apart from relationships with others. And with that One, who is the mysterious center of our existence – intimate yet transcendent – God himself.

Perhaps you have found that there are times in your life when you had precious little left – maybe nothing at all – no energy to summon, no reserves upon which to draw. And yet, at such a time of emptiness, there was nonetheless One, who was near to sustain you. And who did not despise your broken heart or empty hands stretched out.

There are times when we are all Lazarus.

Act II. Both the rich and the poor man die – and now find their positions reversed in the next world.

From this place of torment, Dives begs for a mere drop of water (just as once Lazarus had begged for a scrap of bread.) And when this is denied, Dives asks Father Abraham (which is a surrogate title for God himself) to send some messenger back to his five brothers on earth, so that they might be warned.

They will repent, Dives argues, if only they receive a divine sign of warning.

Who are these five brothers? Again, you and I are these folks – which is the focal point of the drama.

You – even you, who may be sauntering down some broad road in your life, full of vitality and vigor, with so much of the future still before you. So that you can dismiss all this talk of a mysterious goal and accountability as nothing more than a figment of poetic fancy!

Well, don't expect some messenger from beyond to confirm what Moses and the prophets require. Namely, concern for justice, acts of mercy and compassion. No Marley's ghost will come to warn your Ebenezer Scrooge. No Heavens will open, no sign given.

Why? Because the God whom we know, whom we glimpse most clearly in Jesus Christ, is the One who loves. And who wants hearts that respond in love, and not in fear. Thus, the parable is an ongoing drama – in which we are invited to see ourselves – and to understand the clearly enunciated message of the prophets. We are interdependently linked on this small planet spinning in the vastness of the cosmos, we are responsible for aiding and protecting one another.

Now, don't dismiss this as something routine. This is radical at the root of it. For what will finally sustain the vision that we are all indeed brothers and sisters in this world – and that as members of the human race, we are responsible for one another?

We are responsible, for example, for the tens of thousands of mentally ill homeless, who wander the streets of our cities. And we are not removed from the sweltering masses of impoverished, illiterate, hungry people who form the majority of people on this planet.

What will save us from succumbing to indifference and isolation in a world where compassion and care have become scarce commodities? Will some vague humanism? Will some utilitarian ethic?

Perhaps they may help. But ultimately, only a religious vision will ever persevere, ever underwrite the sanctity of human life; which sees human existence as precious. As that arena, which God, in Jesus, chose to enter into, to suffer and to redeem from within.

If humanity is to survive, it will do so only when it is seen "under God."

The late Robert McNamara, who retired as President of the World Bank and served as Secretary of Defense for both John F. Kennedy and Lyndon Johnson, reminded us that in the so-called fourth world "hundreds of millions of individuals barely survive on the margin of life. A condition so degrading as to insult human dignity.

"We cannot build a secure world upon a foundation of human misery," he cautioned.

The fundamental case is, I believe, the moral one. The whole of human history has recognized the principle that the rich and the powerful have a moral obligation to assist the poor and the weak. This is what the sense of community is all about – any community; the community of the family, the community of the nation, the community of nations themselves.

As Christians, when we partake of Holy communion, we join hands spiritually with brothers and sisters of Christ throughout the entire world. As we gather at Table – and as we ourselves are fed and nurtured by bread broken and wine poured.

And as we do, may the Dives in us beware, the Lazarus in us reaffirm our common need and the five brothers among us hear again the Word, which must be heard.

Prayer: Dear Lord, When I am empty-handed or broken-hearted, comfort me. And when I am full, let me give of my gifts of love, compassion, money, experience, kindness and the knowledge of Thee to better the lives of others.

Amen

BAD NEWS/GOOD NEWS

The classic "bad news/good news" jokes always involve a reversal. Take this one of the jumbo jet flying across the Atlantic. Several hours into the flight, the pilot announces over the intercom: "Ladies and gentlemen, this is your captain speaking. I have some good news and some bad news. First, the bad news: We are lost! Now the good news: We are making excellent time."

Good news/bad news. Life is like that, says the Bible. Checkered, full of contradictions, like the human heart, itself.

The very phrase "good news" in Greek is "Euangelion;" in modern English: "Gospel;" in Anglo-Saxon: "God-spell" (meaning God-story.)

Perhaps, you may have seen a performance of Godspell – which is based on St. Matthew's Gospel – either on stage or on screen. Do you remember the opening scene of this tale of good news?

A cluster of characters all wearing gray sweatshirts are seated on the stage with their backs to the audience. One by one, they arise and stand in the spotlight, revealing the name imprinted on the front of their shirts. And sing, persuasively, of each one's own ideology: Socrates, Plato, St. Thomas Aquinas, Martin Luther, Karl Marx, Nietzsche, Sartre, and Martin Luther King.

Then, in a chorus called "The Tower of Babel," each sings his song simultaneously with others. But, as this melodious babel (a clamor of noisy confusion) concludes, down the aisle suddenly appears a modern-day John the Baptist. He blows a ram's horn and then begins to sing to them over and over again. In a moving and hauntingly beautiful melody, he offers his one sentence message: "Prepare ye the way of the Lord!"

And soon, they're all joining in singing and dancing, following this baptizer with his clown-like pail of water and big sponge.

Well, the original John, an itinerant preacher who subsisted on a diet of locusts and wild honey, was scarcely a lovable master of ceremonies. His message is one of warning and doom: the day is coming. The fire will burn and destroy -- and the inauthentic sons of Abraham will flee like insects from the approach of the burning stubble. The woodsman -- finding the unproductive tree, on which he must pay tax, rests for a moment while he doffs his cloak – then, hacks away, hewing roots and all. Or, the whole harvest is pitched into the air -- the heavier grain (the true Israel) falls safely to the ground. But the chaff is blown away, gone with the wind.

For John, things are either black or white; there is no middle path. Either you're in the band that is ready for the coming Messiah – or you're not – and that's it! And, John says, that he's just the advance man; here to get things ready for the real candidate who will bring judgment on the wicked and vindication to the righteous.

John the Baptist has always been an ambiguous figure. We're attracted by his forcefulness and yet, turned-off, repelled by his stern visage and his bad-news message. But bearers of bad news have never been popular.

Just as tyrannical ancient kings often beheaded messengers who brought bad news ("don't shoot the messenger,") the press is often attacked because it is too negative. Some folk would like to throttle those, whose reports challenge the veracity of official views of things. Indeed, there is something in us all, which perennially avoids bad news.

Even the staid Wall Street Journal editorialized on whether most American families were more concerned about nuclear war or getting a Cabbage Patch Kid in time for Christmas. The Journal smugly claimed that about 99% of us worried more about getting one of the dolls than about ultimate destruction.

But we cannot be whole without facing bad news about ourselves. At times, about our strengths that get carried into weakness; about our assertiveness or indifference which places unreasonable strains upon our relationships; about our attempts to purchase security at the price of being closed and cool.

And we cannot be restored, until we hear news that we don't want to hear – about something which has gone wrong in our body, in our system – so also, in our total existence.

Bad news/good news forms a kind of dialectic. Which is why American writer and theologian, Frederick Buechner, in his series of lectures entitled, *The Gospel as Tragedy, Comedy & Fairy Tale,* writes:

"The gospel is bad news before it is good news. It is the news that man is a sinner, to use the old word, that he is evil in the imagination of his heart. That when he looks in a mirror all in a lather, what he sees is at least eight parts chicken, phony, slob."

In the 50th anniversary issue of Esquire, the magazine focused on 50 persons who had shaped contemporary life. Arthur Schlesinger wrote of Reinhold Niebuhr's great contribution to political thought: "The plight of the self," wrote Niebuhr "is that it cannot do the good that it intends." Adds Schlesinger: "For man's pretensions to reason and virtue," he argues, "are ineradicably tainted by self-interest and self-love. Original sin lies in man's illusion that his inherent finiteness and weakness can be overcome. Overweening self-pride vitiates all human endeavor and brings evil into history."

Without that bad news, there is no hope to check human pretensions to perfectibility. But I'm afraid that in popular versions of Christianity – which moralize the tragic depth of the human predicament – very often, people get the impression that the gospel is bad news, rather than good news.

It is true – as the American writer John Barth puts it in one of his novels: "Self knowledge is always bad news!" But that's only part of the truth. The gospel is not about us – about men and women and our sins. It is about God and His love.

Still, some people must evidently believe that the Christian life is such a dull, drab and miserable existence; that none in their right minds would be attracted, unless scared into it. They never get beyond John the Baptist to Jesus Christ and the gospel; that the Peaceable Kingdom is, in some sense, already here, already happening.

What is that good news? Well, let me turn to a remarkable Catholic interpreter of the faith, Andrew Greeley. A priest, a prolific writer and sociologist, Dr. Greeley writes:

"Men (and presumably women) have always suspected, or at least hoped, that God might be good, might even love us."

In the Parable of the Prodigal Son -- which Jesus told to his disciples, the Pharisees and others -- a father has two sons. The younger son asks for his inheritance and goes off. But he loses his fortune (the word prodigal means "wastefully extravagant") and becomes destitute. The son returns home, with the intention of begging his father to be made one of his hired servants; expecting that his relationship with his father is likely severed.

But the father welcomes him back and celebrates his return, for he was lost and now is found!

Dr. Greeley continued, "The Loving Father does not even give the prodigal son time to finish his nicely rehearsed statement of sorrow. The son has barely begun before he is embraced, clothed in a new robe and propelled into a festive banquet.

"The message responds to the most basic and agonizing question that faces all who are part of the human condition: Is everything going to be all right in the end? Jesus' response was quite literally to say: 'You bet your life it is.'"

That is the good news. That is all that we, in the Christian church have to offer. It is all that we have ever had to offer. But it speaks to our needs more than anything else.

Throughout all our wondering, throughout our own indictment of ourselves, comes the words in John 3:16 – which are just what we need to hear: "For God so loved the world, that He gave His only begotten Son; that whosoever believeth in Him will not perish, but have everlasting life."

Prayer: Dear God, let me come home to the shelter of your love.

Amen

BROKEN BREAD

"And He took bread, and gave thanks, and broke it and gave unto them, saying, This is my body which is given for you: this do in remembrance of me."

Those words from Luke 22:19 NKJV have rolled through all the long centuries since. Even today, when we celebrate the sacrament of Holy Communion, they are spoken again. And the question is: do we recognize Him here, in this particular activity? When the loaf is broken and the cup poured out, do we sense something of the very ongoing activity of God in our lives?

The act of breaking – and the act of offering – of emptying and pouring out speak of the pattern in which we encounter His Presence. The living mysterious One, who shares our common life in all of its depth and grandeur.

You and I may come to recognize that Presence most fully, not at times perhaps of triumph. But at times we plod along, aware only of our numbness, our experience of emptiness. Or, in those moments when we open up to ourselves or when we open our lives – however tentatively – to one another. When we allow ourselves to speak the truth about who we really are and what we are enduring.

Sometimes, it is only in our brokenness that we most reveal to others – or to ourselves – our deepest identity. The most profound clues to our essential being. "This is my body which is broken for you --- this do in remembrance of me …."

"We must, each one of us, remember in our own lives," writes American writer and theologian Frederick Buechner, "someone died whom we loved and needed. And from somewhere, something came to fill our emptiness and mend us where we were broken. Was it only time that mended, only the surging busyness of life that filled our emptiness?

"In anger, we said something once that we could have bitten our tongues for afterwards. Or, in anger, somebody said something to us. But out of somewhere, forgiveness came. A bridge was rebuilt. Or maybe forgiveness never came, and to this day we have no bridge back to that friendship.

"Is the human heart the only source of its own healing?

"Is it the human conscience only that whispers to us that in bitterness and estrangement is death?

"We listen to the evening news with its usual recital of shabbiness and horror. And God, if we believe in Him at all, seems remote and powerless, a child's dream.

"But there are other times – often the most unexpected, unlikely times – deeper than shabbiness and horror and at the very heart of darkness, a light unutterable.

"Is it only the unpredictable fluctuations of the human spirit that we have to thank?"

Here, at the Communion table, we are led to say, <u>no</u>. We recognize Another – and ourselves. For we have all experienced brokenness – and here we remember that He was broken, for our sakes.

We have been empty at times – and we remember that he chose to empty himself of all glory and become a servant. To become obedient unto death, even death on a cross.

At the Table – at some level far deeper than the poor power of words can convey – we find, in broken bread and wine poured (such common things) new life, new strength, healing and hope.

He is known to us and to others in the breaking of the bread.

He is known, too, when we find ourselves and our lives broken. When things go wrong, very wrong. When we are defeated, or afraid that we are defeated. When we have been badly abused and hurt. When we have sinned and know it. When we are forced to admit that we have failed.

But it is then – in the midst of our small deaths and broken spirits – that strangely, God can bring a sense of renewal, peace and acceptance.

It is here that we can learn to speak of Jesus Christ in the present tense, as One who is with us. Who brings a presence into the empty places of our lives.

At the Table, we receive, in the words of the ancient liturgy, "refreshing and rest unto our souls …"

And then what? Then we are asked – in the experience of new life and new strength – to be willing to be broken open in a new way. To be willing to be emptied in a new way. To give of ourselves, our efforts, our time, our imagination, our money. Not in simple self-seeking, but in self-giving -- which strangely leads to self-fulfillment and enhancement.

That's why Christians are always in mission – always emptying themselves. Always moving to tell or to show someone some good news. To bring some hope, to bind up some wounds, to advocate the things which lead to human dignity for all the children of God.

We do so, not in a grim or joyless way. But confidently, that the One whom we recognize here – in the breaking of the bread – will take what we have to offer. And make it significant for His purposes in our day and generation.

Playwright George Bernard Shaw, in the long preface to his play, *Androcles and the Lion* commented about the Gospel according to Matthew:

"Matthew then tells how after three days, an angel opened the family vault of Joseph, a rich man of Arimathea, where Jesus was buried. Whereupon, Jesus rose and returned from Jerusalem to Galilee and resumed his preaching with his disciples. Assuring them that He would be with them to the end of the world."

Then Shaw added, "at that point the narrative abruptly stops. The story has no ending."

"The story has no ending …." No, it goes on.

It goes on whenever we are, like the bread and wine, broken open, emptied. That we may be made fed and made full. That we may experience what millions through years have found, "He was known to them in the breaking of the bread …."

Prayer: When I am broken and empty, help me to see myself and Thee more clearly.

Amen

CALLED TOGETHER

Alfred Whitehead, that great philosopher of the 20th century, who helped to foster a whole new relationship between science and religion, once declared that "religion is what the individual does with his own aloneness." And that is true, of course. In the sense that just as no one else can breathe for you, or fall in love for you, or walk for you, so no else can believe for you.

There are some things – some very basic things – that must be done by each of us, alone. And we have it from spiritual authorities as diverse as the 14th Century monk, Thomas à Kempis to 20th Century Swedish diplomat and economist, Dag Hammarskjöld: that there is a loneliness, which is woven into the very fabric of religious experience. The attempt to come to grips with the mystery and meaning of who you are is always solitary work.

But that's only half the truth. The other half is that for those of us nurtured in the Judaic-Christian tradition, religion isn't so much ultimately what you do with your aloneness. It's what you do with your neighbors, yourself and your God.

Do unto others as you would have them do unto you.

One hears that note again and again in the New Testament. For example, Saint Peter told the early Christian community that they were a chosen race, a royal priesthood, a holy nation. God's own people, that they may declare the wonderful deeds of Him who called them out of darkness into His marvelous light. Once, they were no people, but now they are God's people ….

This sense of community is always in danger of being eroded and lost. We live in a mass society, which tends to produce an anonymous world. Which diminishes the personal, the communal, those forces, which, naturally bind us together. Indeed, ironically, the very advancements in technology, in communication systems, which one might assume would strengthen community, often does just the opposite.

Some years ago, the British scientist/novelist, C.P. Snow warned that we no longer had one culture, but two – and the two were moving dangerously apart, having less and less to do with each other. One culture was that informed by the high religions and the humanities; the other was the scientific and technical.

Technology, of course, can be used – and continues to be used – for either good or evil. But in itself, it is absolutely amoral, without values. Values are derived ultimately from community, from consensus, from interaction among people in a network of responsibility and care.

Today, community is threatened by a subtle, but very real phenomenon. The emergence of technically brilliant people, who for all intents and purposes – are unaffected by the values created and sustained by the high religions.

These competent technicians often have no commitment to anything beyond the demonstration of their own technical competency. Seem to know nothing of sacrificing any of their time, talents, and efforts on behalf of another human being. And are seemingly so absorbed in themselves and technology, without any ethical or psychological ballast to link them with the highest expression of human community.

And with today's ubiquitous use of personal technology, what with cell phones and apps and watches and notepads, doesn't this describe us all? To quote Walt Kelly from his well-loved Pogo cartoon strip, "we have met the enemy and he is us."

Consider the case of a brilliant, handsome, young architect, Albert Speer, the pure technician, who gave himself over to the service of Adolph Hitler. And whose technical genius was such that he probably was able to keep the cruel, Nazi war machine going for an extra year.

In prison, he mused about his life and said. "I saw no moral ground outside the system … I never gave my existence or reason-for-being, a thought."

He may, unfortunately, represent the emerging men and women of our age.

Also of German ancestry, whose father was incarcerated for his Jewish heritage, Dr. Steven Muller, a Rhodes Scholar, culminated a brilliant career as President Emeritus of Johns Hopkins University and Hospital with:

"The biggest failing in higher education today is that we fall short in exposing students to values. We don't really provide a value framework to young people who more and more are searching for it. Since World War II, we've seen the greatest disintegration of social consensus and the most accelerated pace and degree of change in human history. As a result, all of our institutions have lost a coherent set of values – including universities.

"The failure to rally around a set of values means that universities are turning out potentially highly skilled barbarians. People who are very expert in the laboratory or at the computer or in surgery or in the courtroom, but who have no real understanding of their own society."

Now, it is in this kind of world that Christians today are summoned to be God's own people, God's priests. And I believe in what happens in worship, where the Word of God is preached and enacted in sacraments. Where people hold one another and the world before God in common prayer and concern. An urgently needed antidote to the impact of a mass society, which robs the world of a sense of community and values.

Thus, we Christians have a special vocation: to bear witness to the love of God for all people. And as disciples of Jesus Christ, to embody that love and try to show it to the world. Which means, of course, engaging the world using the best resources that God has given us – our minds, our talents, our money, our energy, and our technology.

For the only resource in a world that is suffering from the erosion of values, which affirms and defends individual human worth, is to be serious and influential about God's love for all people. It means taking our calling more seriously than we have.

In his final Christmas sermon, the late Episcopal pastor of Boston, Theodore Parker Ferris preached,

"We all have, some more than others, a tendency to go off in a corner by ourselves. There are times when we want to be alone, we want to be left alone, we need to be alone.

"If we are in trouble, we want to shed our tears in private, nurse our own wounds by ourselves. Be bitter if we want to be, be stony-faced against the world ….

"But you don't get very far alone. If you cut yourself off from the rest of your human family … go into a corner and sulk in private or destroy others in public protest.

"You can't do it yourself. You must join hands with the ones who can help you – a doctor, a nurse, a friend. And you can join hands with God, in prayer."

In a world where the sense of human worth is threatened. Where people are cut off from one another with vast forces and fear. The Christian community needs to take seriously its call to be the people of God. A holy race, bearing witness to the sanctity of life shown forth in the very human face of a Man from Nazareth.

Prayer: Oh Lord, help me use my God-given gifts to show His love to all people.

Amen

CHARIOTS OF FIRE

It was what people in the industry called a "sleeper." Here was an unpretentious little British film about two young athletes, who win gold medals for their country in the Olympic Games of 1924.

Now, what kind of chance for commercial success does a film like that have? After all, it's set so long ago. And it's about people, who are the opposite of all the dominant movie heroes of recent years -- the seekers, the disaffected, the cynical.

But, as you know, *Chariots of Fire* went on to stir audiences and to win an Academy Award for Best Film of 1981.

The film was about winning, of course. But, it was about something more than that, too. It was about motivation. What is it that drives a person to overcome the barriers of boredom, pain and peer pressure to feel the pleasure of streaking across the tape?

As Eric Liddell says in his soft Lowland Scots voice: "It's within you."

Eric Liddell was a Scottish Presbyterian. He was a twenty-two year old university science major, who felt a call to follow his father into China as a missionary.

He was also an international star as a rugby player and one of the fastest runners ever produced by Scotland.

His family was not confident in his desire to run in the Olympic Games, fearing that it might get in the way of his missionary preparation.

Eric tells his sister that he is totally committed to God. But, he adds with a grin, "God made me fast." And he resolved to run and to win to the "glory of God." That was the fire within him.

Harold Abrahams is the other main character. Within him, too, burned a consuming fire.

And a fire in the soul has ultimately to do with what we call religion. Harold Abrahams' fire was ignited by bigotry. He was Jewish. And despite all the privileges of an expensive education in England's venerable and exclusive schools, he sensed and suffered from that polite and subtle anti-Semitism. Which can be as wounding as a pogrom or a violent riot and rape.

So, while enjoying all the amenities and delights of a Cambridge college; Harold dedicates himself, with every fiber of his being, to train, to run and to win.

Winning was "showing them." The God of Harold Abrahams was the God of Abraham and although not outwardly a practicing believer, he had the ancestral fires burning within.

Both young men stand their ground with integrity, struggle against pressure to compromise -- and win! In both, the fires burn deep within.

Somewhere in the movie, we hear a choir singing Parry's setting of William Blake's "Jerusalem." The poem is based on a legend that Jesus once came to England. Its climax is the burning resolve to create the Jerusalem of God out of the grim conditions in England's industrial revolution.

> "Bring me my Bow of burning gold!
> Bring me my Arrows of desire
> Bring me my spear: O clouds, unfold!
> Bring me my Chariot of fire
>
> I will not cease from Mental Flight,
> Nor shall my Sword sleep in my hand,
> Till we have built Jerusalem,
> In England's green and pleasant Land."

That was a visionary hymn of a society transformed by the Kingdom of God.

Blake's phrase "Chariot of fire" (the title of the film) refers to the story of the prophet Elijah passing his mantle to Elisha before leaving him for Heaven.

The old proverb has it right. "Without a vision, the people perish."

And vision means something -- which flames, which transcends -- the ordinary. And beckons a deep response.

Where are our chariots of fire today? Where do you find a source for your commitment to something more than your own brilliance or competence or narrow self-interest?

In the movie, there is a scene (before we are taken to the Olympic Stadium) of Eric Liddell preaching from the pulpit of the Scottish Church in Paris.

"He gives power to the faint, and to them who have no strength, He increases might. But they that wait upon the Lord, shall renew their strength. They shall mount up with wings as eagles, they shall run and not be weary …"

Now, that is visionary. That is religion with wings, religion that soars. Words first spoken to people in exile in Babylon, promising power, which the world could not see.

That is prophetic vision – vision that allows us to see something more than the obvious power by which people continue to push and pull to get their way. There is another power. A power, which comes from within. A power, which is not external and coercive, but affective. A power, which moves us to love.

How can we learn what it means to "wait upon the Lord" so that we can "mount up with wings as eagles…so that we can run and not be weary?"

Clearly, one way to "renew our strength," is worship. But it must be worship to which we come expectantly, in which we share actively. Entered not upon ourselves, but upon the One, who stoops to serve. Whom Jesus taught us to call, "Father."

The real test of a soaring faith comes not with passing vision. But with the practical plodding loyalty of those, who stand by their convictions outside the premises of a church or synagogue, where commitment is tested.

And who knows where that will lead? Well, nobody knows for sure.

Both young men lived out their convictions. Harold Abrahams went on to marry into the British aristocracy and died respected and honored. Eric Liddell went to China as a missionary and died in a Japanese internment camp at Weihsien in occupied China.

American theologian, Langdon Brown Gilkey wrote a jaundiced account of the life inside that compound -- in which people of all ages and backgrounds – lived in boredom and misery. In his account, there is hardly a good word for anyone – least of all for Protestant Christians. But then, you turn the page and find these words: "It is rare indeed, when anyone has the good fortune to meet a saint. But he (Eric Liddell) comes as close to it as anyone I have ever known."

Liddell was living out his faith. He befriended the prostitute and the despised businessman, carried coal for the weak and taught the young. Got ready to sell his gold watch and tore up his sheets for bandages.

Thus, we glimpse the chariots of fire and an unpretentious man, who used his gifts to the glory of God in the most simple of ways. And yet he is still the same Eric, in a multi-colored shirt made of old curtains and looking extremely ordinary and nothing special at all.

In her biography, *The Flying Scotsman*, author Sally Magnusson wrote, "Perhaps it wouldn't be too fanciful, either, to suppose that the sancta simplicitas -- the sacred simplicity – of a man like Eric Liddell will continue to reverberate gently down the years. And affect all sorts of unlikely people. The secret of that charisma of his, still touching people from the 1920's schoolgirl to the 1980's filmmaker has to be his faith. Though that may be too simple an answer for our times. It has to be something to do with the resources he tapped when his head jerked back in a race and he ran blind. Something to do with the spiritual source he surrendered to when the fighting was over. Whatever his secret, it will be found there, where the joy and the pain and the love were greatest.

"If that is too simple an answer for an age that tends to be more comfortable with the unresolved paradox of a life that comprehends both drive and serenity; will to achieve and grace to give in; ordinariness and charisma – then it's probably a comment on us.

"For in the end, there is really no paradox, no enigma about Eric Liddell's life. Wasn't it (Scottish poet Robert) Burns who said, that a simple man is 'a problem that puzzles the devil?'"

In a world, where the quality of life is deeply at stake, where the future of the planet, and the race which inhabits it, is up for grabs, where is the vision? Where are the people who are summoned?

Prayer: Here I am Lord. Light a fire in my soul that I may do Thy will.

Amen

CONTRADICTIONS OF A NEW YEAR

Every calendar New Year or birthday seems always to be a time for reflection – for self-scrutiny, for measuring performance against expectations.

And I suppose – no matter how each one of us adds things up for ourselves, no matter what resolutions we bravely make, we sense again the fact that our lives are always full of contradictions.

A certain Mr. Jones inadvertently spoke of this during a rough ocean crossing, when he was suffering severe motion sickness. During one of the more unsettled periods, he was leaning over the rail retching miserably, when a kindly steward patted him on the shoulder. "Oh, I know, Sir," said the steward, "that it seems truly awful. But just remember, no man ever died of seasickness!"

Jones lifted his green countenance to the steward's concerned face and gasped: "For Heaven's sake, man, don't say that. It's only the wonderful hope of dying that's keeping me alive."

Such are the contradictions of life.

From time immemorial, men and women have tried to point to the mysterious meaning of life. In great sagas, in poems, in narrative chronologies, life is portrayed as a setting out, a journey to distant places, along unknown paths. Ralph Waldo Emerson wrote: "Do not go where the path may lead, go instead where there is no path and leave a trail."

Psychologist Eugene Kennedy puts it: "Even in the legends of King

Arthur, we discover a reflection of this. The knights are in pursuit of the Grail; it is clear, however, that the effort to find the Grail, is more important than the actual discovery. Success is a journey, not a destination.

"The legends tell that each knight had to leave the Round Table and "enter the forest at its darkest part."

That's where each of us must enter too.

"Start where you are, use what you have, do what you can," observed Arthur Ashe. He was the first and only African-American male tennis player to be ranked No. 1 in the world and win the U.S. Open and Wimbledon.

"The best way to judge a life is to ask yourself," he continued, "did I make the best use of the time I had? From what we get, we can make a living. What we give, however, makes a life."

And any Trekker will recite the text spoken at the beginning of many Star Trek television episodes and films from 1966 onward: "Space: the final frontier … to boldly go where no man has gone before."

Each of us ends life at a place where no one has quite gone before. Each one of us comes with certain graces and certain gifts: these cannot be tested, nor can you even grasp their meaning, unless you are willing to cut your own path.

American theologian, Frederick Buechner writes: "The place God calls you to is the place where your deep gladness and the world's deep hunger meet."

The unique meaning of life is revealed to the men and women, who are not afraid to find their own way. The great myths of humanity are those stories, which we eventually live out in our own lives. So, in a real sense, we are all standing by that darkest part of the forest, that place which we must enter by ourselves, if we are to know ourselves and find each other.

The journey toward wholeness is not made by looking away from our true selves – but actively accepting our own, individual different journeys to personhood. Trust that power, which is able to help make sense of it. That power is God's love, which can help us live with the contradictions and yet -- retain a sense of personal, vigorous hope.

You and I must take our own various, individual journeys. No one else can walk your way for you. And yet, none of us really walks alone. We are surrounded by a "great cloud of witnesses" – fellow travelers, if you will.

The Christian life isn't one of stoic isolation – but is rather one of friendship, comradeship, in which our identities are shaped and shared with others, who walk along the way. Thus, the journey then becomes a pilgrimage – in which we are able to support, to help one another.

Time and time again, I am struck by the power, which can come when we tell someone else, no matter how tentatively, something about our real journey – the sense of our fears, our longings, our vulnerabilities, our uncertainties in the face of contradictions. And when we are heard – or when someone shares with us something of his or her journey in return, we are mutually encouraged, mutually strengthened.

It is true, of course, that we can and do lose our way. Or become so discouraged (which literally means without courage) that we curse the fact that we ever set out on the journey in the first place.

Sometimes – in this contradictory life we lead – we discover that inexplicably; we haven't made progress at all, but have actually fallen back. We are shocked sometimes, when we discover that something inside, long thought to have been extinguished, can suddenly be fanned to life again by some seemingly trivial incident.

The problem – whether it is anger, envy, lust, whatever – may lay sleeping in the embers, sometimes for years. And it is hard to say why – after this long time – it should suddenly stir to brightness once more.

One parishioner wrote: "When I woke up, all the hurts and misunderstandings and resentments I had ever experienced during my life – things I hadn't thought about recently or in years – came surging to the surface ..."

This, however, is part of the human journey – and although it may disturb us to find ourselves falling back, it cannot be denied. Worst of all, is to be put down for it. It doesn't help for self-righteous people, moralizers, to call out epithets at others, such as "backslider" or worse. People, who find themselves in a fix, generally have all the self-judgment they can possibly handle.

There are times, when we simply don't understand our own journeys; there are times, when we are caught off guard and off balance by the contradictory experiences of life. But don't panic. This, too, is part of the human condition – and in Jesus Christ, God claims the whole of the human condition – its contradictions, its ambiguities, its frustrations and failures.

He does not condemn us, when we wander off into self-defeating behaviors. He does not reject us, when we feel overwhelmed by obstacles and contradictions.

Rather – He loves us – and by that love, entices us to start again, to walk with new hope. And to know that there are new possibilities and new redemptive opportunities, even in contradictory situations.

This is good news! We don't have to pretend to have it all together. We don't have to feign some kind of perfectionist image of ourselves, which denies the contradictions -- the false starts of our journeys. We can accept ourselves in the full range of our humanity, because we are loved and accepted beyond ourselves.

With that knowledge, hopefully in this New Year, we can be a little kinder to ourselves. And a little kinder, too, to those fellow pilgrims, who stumble at times and need some kind of helping gesture from us. In a life journey filled with contradictions, isn't that the best way to walk?

Prayer: Lord, help me welcome the contradictions in my life and the uniqueness I bring to the world.

Amen

COPING WITH GRIEF

In 1789, when the fledgling American republic was entering a new phase in its life, Benjamin Franklin wrote these words to a friend in Paris: "Our constitution is in actual operation. Everything appears to promise that it will last." Then, with tongue-in-cheek or with fingers crossed, he added this qualification: "But in this world, nothing is certain but death and taxes."

The phrase stuck somehow in our consciousness – and we use it at times, in a kind of ironic way to try to defend ourselves against the unpredictability we experience in life. The only certainties – death and taxes. Well, we seem to say with a shrug, what can you expect from life anyway?

But death is a reality, which we can never easily shrug off. It is a painfully real and sober reality. We are living up life towards the goal of death.

Comedian Woody Allen jokes, "I'm not afraid to die, I just don't want to be there when it happens." And baseball great, Yogi Berra, chimed in with, "Always go to other people's funerals or they won't come to yours."

But how to cope with the reality each of us will inevitably face – sorrow and grief.

For there does come a time in the life of each of us, sooner or later, when profound, soul-wrenching sorrow comes. Whenever we lose someone, whom we have loved and who has loved us. Someone, whom we touched and who, in turn, has touched us and changed us deeply. Then, we experience very deep pain and sorrow.

There are stages to grief and sorrow – and the first one is shock, the numbness that comes because nothing seems real. And we find ourselves going through the motions, as if it were all a bad dream, from which we will surely awake.

But we awake to find the reality there; it dawns upon us that the loss is permanent and real and terrible to bear. And it is here that the **first** practical thing should be said: do not be afraid to release the tension, to express the grief you feel. Upon seeing the grief of Martha and Mary for his death on the cross, the Gospel of John quotes the shortest verse in all Scripture, Jesus wept.

In our society, it may be a hard thing to cry, but it is not a bad thing. Our tears not only express the deep well of our feelings but they also make us one with all who have ever loved and tried to reach out in a tender way to another.

"Our tears," said Charles Dickens "are rain upon the blinding dust of earth, overlaying our hard hearts." But our tears redeem us when they reveal us clearly to another. When we become vulnerable, when we do not shield ourselves from the risk, which is involved in loving and in being very human.

The Apostle Paul – who was no stranger to grief himself – wrote, Grieve not as those who have no hope.

There's the **second** practical thing to be said: remember that God is with you to sustain you, to provide the strength, which you need. Not an easy thing to grasp. But it is as crucial as expressing your grief. Hold onto your faith – even though you may feel as though you're drowning and cannot feel God's presence.

But like Job of old, who was beset on all sides, cried, "I know that my Redeemer lives!" All through the centuries, people who have been able to face grief in the knowledge that God still cares about them say that grief can be counted among the great deepening experiences of life. As the prophet Kahlil Gibran wrote: "the deeper pain carves into your soul, the more joy it can contain."

The basis of your holding on, of clinging to your faith is what God has done in Jesus. For Christ's crucifixion means that he understands suffering from the inside. And His resurrection is assurance that God cannot be finally put down by anything in this world. And that nothing, not even the terrible pain or loss and grief, nothing, can separate us from this love of Jesus Christ.

This is no time to abandon your faith – it is a time to hold onto it, to guard it, however slender the thread, however precarious your grasp. But hold on – and He will see you through, giving you strength sufficient for one moment at a time.

There will be days when everything seems empty, when you feel overwhelmed and very much alone. There will be times when you resent or resist the consolation others offer. Times when you will become indifferent toward life, or angry at the world or with God.

But now and then, perhaps, a small ray of light will come through the dark clouds, now and then the depression will lift and you will receive some token of God's deep healing. And the terrible fog of grief will begin to break up and you can again see tokens of God's care and concern.

And that leads to a **third** practical thing. When the time comes, return to life and pick up those responsibilities, which God has given you. Find a task to do – worthy of your talents – a job that will absorb all your energy in outpouring love. To paraphrase theologian Frederick Buechner, "God's will for my life is that place where my talents meet the needs of the world."

We do not become merely "our old selves again." No – when we go through profound grief, we are different people from then on.

We are stronger, our thoughts go deeper, and we are more equipped to be about the very human business of helping our neighbors. We walk along a very human path and we learn how, in our grief, the presence of another person can bring a certain wholeness to our sorrow. And so we can, in some measure, now become instruments of God's own healing for others.

One of the most helpful messages ever preached was by a Scottish pastor …

"I don't think you need be afraid of life … our hearts are very frail; and there are places where the road is very steep and very lonely. But we have a wonderful God."

And as the Apostle Paul asked his followers, "What can separate us from His love? Not death," he said, immediately pushing aside at once as the most obvious of all impossibilities. "No, not death. For standing in the roaring of the Jordan, cold to the heart with its dreadful chill and very conscious of the terror of its rushing. I, too, can call back to you who one day in your turn will have to cross it. Be of good cheer, my brother, for I feel the bottom and it is sound."

Prayer: Dear Lord, when I face the inevitable sorrows of my life, let me remember: Be of good cheer, for I feel the bottom and it is sound.

Amen

DEALING WITH FEELINGS

Let me share with you a recent conversation about dealing with feelings, those deep parts of ourselves, which we all experience in life.

After a worship service; a young man, well-educated and successful in his profession, said, "You know, Pastor, I understood what you were talking about. The mystery and ambiguity of life, and the fact that the greatest event for Christians, the resurrection, can't ever be grasped fully by logic – only by faith.

"And that's all right. But it hasn't been easy for me to come to. And the reason is that I've always trusted logic, sequence, order, and rationality. And, conversely, I've always distrusted my feelings. Putting them down, being embarrassed by them, feeling that, somehow; they really weren't as valid or trustworthy as the rational part of me. But now, in therapy, I'm beginning to experience a kind of resurrection of myself. It's becoming all right to trust my feelings; it's okay to acknowledge them and to risk a little by expressing them to others."

I share this to illustrate the problem for so many of us: our feelings. Feelings can seem strange creatures – and we don't know what to do with them – or, more accurately, what they will do with us.

Feelings can frighten us. They take us to places where we no longer have control, and the fine line between rationality and irrationality dissolves. After all, we've been taught over and over that mature people should always be in control of ourselves. And that if you go about expressing your emotions and your feelings openly, then somehow you are not quite respectable or grown up.

Now, obviously, there is the question always of when to express feelings appropriately and how to express them. But to constantly deny, repress or suppress our feelings is to surrender something of our own humanity and; indeed, in some ways to threaten our lives.

Repress feelings and strange things happen: The person who denies anger and frustration at work will manifest it at home.

The person who suppresses feelings, who denies them because they are so ugly or so threatening and shameful, can find those very feelings – unventilated – turning back upon one's own body. Leading to physical illness and pain – pain which is very, very real, but which is emotionally-based.

Or the person, who is convinced that somehow it is wrong to experience all the contradictory feelings and emotions and, who tries to rise above them – may well be on the way to a mental breakdown.

Emotions are simply that powerful.

But where did we get the idea that feelings are <u>wrong</u> to have and therefore, <u>wrong</u> to admit to, to own, to express?

Well, that notion is deeply embedded in our culture. You can hear it expressed in all kinds of popular aphorisms: If a person is down, he is told to pick himself up. "Pull yourself together," we say.

Early in life, we hear that "big boys don't cry," or "little girls aren't supposed to be aggressive." Or, if we face some grief, some loss; we are supposed to keep our chins up, remain composed, trust God and go on. As if nothing has really happened to us.

Actually, that is a model that comes from classical antiquity. The Greeks had the notion that some of a person's facilities were superior and some were inferior, demanding subordination and repression.

To be a mature person – was to be, above all things, rational. And to pit that divine spark of reason against the chaotic forces within oneself: the emotions, appetites, desires.

Unfortunately, much of Christianity absorbed this notion; and developed an ethic of control, in which the child-like elements were to be suppressed or denied. In which, if one really led the good Christian life, one was always composed, maintained one's balance with equanimity and poise and never betrayed those darker impulses of fear, anger, doubt, distress.

I find great irony in this. For even a cursory reading of the four Gospels of the Bible shows that the Founder of Christianity, the Pioneer of our Faith -- Jesus of Nazareth, experienced and expressed the full range of human feelings and emotions. He did not deny or repress them. Yet we say that we glimpse in Him the very mystery of God, himself. And, at the same time, the full realization of authentic human life, or what it means to be truly human and fully alive.

For example, at one point in His ministry, Jesus told his disciples in John 16:33:

"In me, ye might have peace. In the world, ye shall have tribulation. But be of good cheer; I have overcome the world."

What is the feeling, which those words convey? Well … joy, triumph, elation.

But at another time in His ministry, after many of His disciples drew back and no longer went about with Him, Jesus asked whether the twelve would also go away?"

What is the feeling behind these words? Well … sadness, abandonment, wistfulness, defeat.

The Jesus, who walked the dusty roads of Galilee. Who intensely interacted with all kinds of people from all walks of life. Who, finally suffered and died the worst kind of death imaginable in the Roman world, experienced the whole gamut of human feelings from a to z.

He experienced joy, success, sorrow, anger, tenderness, forsakenness, fear and despair. He was fully human, and he showed us the ultimate meaning of human life by living out a love; which embraced the full range of heights and depths of the human experience.

Let me now, in the light of the life of Jesus Christ, suggest how we might deal with the fundamental problem of feelings.

First, we need to accept our feelings as a valid part of our true human experience. As an integral part of ourselves – and not be panicked by them. We do not have to pretend to be more than our Lord. We can accept ourselves – we can allow ourselves to fear, to grieve, to rejoice, to celebrate, to doubt, to be angry.

Yes, of course, there is always risk in expressing feelings. None of us surely would deny that. But there is a greater risk in not expressing feelings; of not seeing that they are part of our wholeness as human beings.

We can accept them in the certainty that they do have something important to contribute to us. That if we listen to our feelings, try to hear what they are saying to us, we will not be diminished, but enhanced.

For our feelings come from the roots of our being, from our depths – and reveal something basic about ourselves to ourselves. About those things that disturb us, about those things of which we feel secure and certain, about those things for which we might even make sacrifices. We need to accept our feelings – and be instructed by them.

Second, we need to hear then, the good news of the gospel. Which is addressed to the whole person – and not just part of us. The good news is that God loves us – as we are. He does not just love us when we are in control, when we are composed, when we are positive or pious. He loves us unconditionally; that is what the cross is all about. He sealed that love with his own blood.

He loves us unconditionally – and sets his affections upon us whether we are ebullient or depressed, up or down.

And He calls us to deal compassionately with ourselves – and with others. To love ourselves and our neighbors, as He loves us. And that means that we accept our brothers and sisters, in their joys and their doubts. That we try – as best we can by our presence -- to let them express their fears and anxieties. To let them have their feelings, rightly or wrongly. And look together for the strength of Christ, who is with us in our checkered, never dull, process of growing and becoming more fully human.

Prayer: Let me be fully alive, acknowledging all of the feelings that teach me what I need to know about myself and about being a human being.

Amen

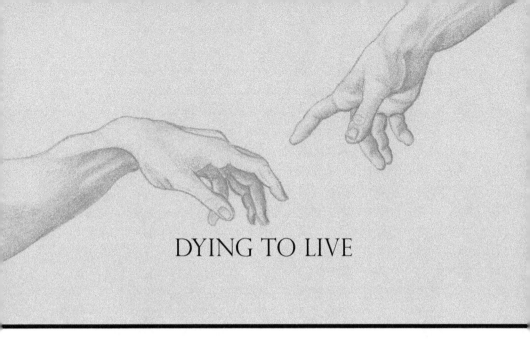

DYING TO LIVE

Before her death from breast cancer at age 63, Chief Justice Rose Bird of the California Supreme Court spoke about the significant impact, which cancer and its recurrence had upon her.

"In a peculiar way, death can teach you what life is all about," she told a community forum in Los Angeles. "It's a painful lesson and a difficult journey. But I am personally grateful that I was made to travel this path at a relatively early age. For I have learned much about myself, much about what I want out of life and much about how precious life and people are.

"It is our relationships with others; especially those whom we love, that give the fullest meaning to life. I don't think I ever really knew that, emotionally or intellectually, until my second bout with cancer."

An event occurs – and perspectives are forever different. So with Jesus' paradoxical statement in Matthew 16:25 "Whosoever will save his life shall lose it, and whosoever will lose his life for my sake, shall find it."

Through all this shines a basic truth about your life and mine. We are all made for allegiance to a higher life; and real life eludes us until we live in this respectful deference.

In the 4th Century, Saint Augustine of Hippo said it when he cried out, "Thou hast made us for Thyself, O Lord, and our heart is restless, until we rest in Thee."

Former President Barack Obama's favorite philosopher, outspoken

Protestant pastor Reinhold Niebuhr put it this way. "Human personality is so constructed that it must be possessed, if it is to escape the prison of self possession. The self must be possessed from beyond itself."

There is a cleft deep in our nature. There are only two roads to travel in life: the road of self-centeredness or the road of moving away from that, even if you are merely dragged along in an outward direction.

Now, in an age, when we all succumb to the siren call to indulgence and security. When the "Me Generation" continues to be preoccupied by endless contemplation of itself through a myriad of alleged therapies and techniques, talk of self-denial seems heretical – scandalous, defying the accepted wisdom of the age.

Self-expression alone, self-indulgence per se, is glorified. Mass society, the impact of technology, economic dislocation, the poverty of political choice reinforce the movement of the self within a constricted circle. And yet, human life can only be fulfilled in a dynamic relationship. In that tension and interplay in which the self is committed to that, which is beyond itself.

One of the best-known newspaper editors of the 20th Century, the late Arthur Brisbane said prophetically: "The psychology of modern times has turned man's mind too much on himself."

Based on the old Greek admonition, 'know thyself,' it has encouraged and overemphasized the introspective, know yourself, discover yourself!

But men and women have never done that. They come into the world weeping and go out of it wondering, and never seem to fathom the depths of the self. Perhaps, it is no part of the Divine plan to have us fully know ourselves. That knowledge would make us lose interest in our work, the more important creative work, which we were put here to do. A healthier approach than know thyself is the Christian one: give thyself, deny thyself, lose thyself.

This is the wisdom, which we've forgotten in our recurring crises of identity, in our search for self-actualization. We find our true selves only when somehow, we get ourselves out of the center and put some higher loyalty there. Only when we move from a self-preoccupied life to a God-centered life. Or at least, in the tension of those two polarities.

Such learned men as these have said it.

Theoretical physicist Albert Einstein: "Only a life lived for others is worthwhile."

Philosopher Albert Camus: "If, after all, men cannot always make history have a meaning; they can always act so that their own lives have one."

British novelist, C. S. Lewis: "To love at all is to be vulnerable. Love anything and your heart will certainly be wrung and possibly broken. If you want to make sure of keeping it intact, you must give your heart to none …avoid all entanglements, lock it up safe in a casket of selfishness."

But in that casket – safe, dark, motionless, airless – it will change. It will not be broken – it will become unbreakable, impenetrable, and irredeemable.

It is costly to love – to move out of the self's beguiling circle; but it is ultimately more costly not to love.

I do not know – nor can I presume – what seeking the Kingdom of God, the way of love, may mean for you. Where you live amidst the tensions and ambiguities and opportunities and occasions of your life.

But I do know this: you have an opportunity, a chance and a challenge to minister in your own life – as surely as I do in mine.

And I know this: that those who follow Jesus Christ are surely called upon – as his first disciples were – to give to the wider community those qualities which are desperately needed by people today. And what are they?

These, for instance:

As Christians, you are called to give of your belief – no matter how imprecisely reasoned it may be – to the person around you, who has lost faith in him or herself, in life, in God.

As Christians, you are called to give of whatever measure of hope you have to the person, who has given up on finding any good, anywhere at all.

As Christians, you are called to give of your concern and care to those, who think that love is forever beyond them.

As Christians, you are called to be concerned about things public, about the quality of civic life, about issues regarding justice and equity, about those, who are powerless and voiceless.

And as you respond – you will not be diminished – but enhanced, made more fully you.

That is the way of Christ, who – like the bread and the wine – was himself broken open for us, poured out that we may receive life. Emptied, he triumphed. Dying, he lived. And lives still to those, who have ears to hear and eyes, to see.

Prayer: Dear Lord, let me live in the light of He who died for me.

Amen

FACING OUR OWN TRAGEDIES

Recently, a friend of mine decided not to read any new or currently popular books. Rather, she turned again to re-read old favorites from the past, classics if you will. And she found that the works of Melville and Ibsen and Tolstoy were actually more powerful and poignant than when she had first read them years ago.

Now, I think the reason for this is obvious. She brings to these great works her own lifetime of experience and a perspective that has been gained at the price of maturity. Her perspective has deepened and changed.

Something like this happened to me, too, when I read again Arthur Millers' great play, *Death of a Salesman*.

As a young seminary student, I had been impressed by its vitality. Now, much older, I've experienced something more of the depths, terrors and resurrections of human existence. I find that I can identify with the main character, Willy Loman, in a new way, an inside and more sympathetic way.

The play is a classic tragedy.

"Tragedy," the Greek philosopher Aristotle told us, "is an imitation of incidents arousing pity and fear." Pity for someone caught in an undeserved misfortune. Fear, because we see that the misfortune is brought on to ones very much like us – not a vicious and depraved person, but someone who makes errors in judgment.

In the preface to his play, Arthur Miller stated that it was his aim to raise the tragedy of the common man to the level of a highly conceived drama.

Let's take a look at this enduring dramatic work.

Willy Loman is a travelling salesman. He has covered the Boston territory for 34 years and now, at 63, finds that he is washed up. He is no longer able to make it. Younger men are taking over. The old man, who hired Willy, has been succeeded in the family business by his son, Howard. And the son has no feeling or regard for loyalty or commitments made years before by his father.

Willy has two sons, Biff and Happy, whom he had idolized during their adolescence, but who have failed him now.

His wife, Linda, is described eloquently by Arthur Miller in the opening stage directions as "most often jovial, she has developed an iron repression of her exceptions to Willy's behavior. She more than loves him, she admires him. As though his mercurial nature, his temper, his massive dreams and little cruelties, served her only as sharp reminders of the turbulent longings within him. Longings which she shares, but lacks the temperament to utter and follow to the end."

Part of the tragedy is Willy's feeling that he has been victimized by the system. He has been paying off the mortgage, borrowing on his insurance, making payments on his household furnishings all his life. And just when he should be able to enjoy them all, he is about to be fired.

When Linda tells him that the refrigerator has broken down, Willy says, "Whoever heard of a Hastings refrigerator? Once in my life, I would like to own something outright before it's broken! I'm always in a race with the junkyard. I just finished paying for the car, and it's on its last legs. The refrigerator consumes belts like a maniac. They time those things. They time them so when you finally have paid for them, they're used up."

The major tragedy is that Willy has never been able to come to terms with himself – or his dreams. Willy's dream has been to be a success, an outstanding success, and he is willing to sacrifice principles and everything else to that dream.

His ideal is a salesman named Dave Singleton – who, when he died at an advanced age, drew hundreds of other salesmen to his funeral.

Willy says ... "Things were sad on a lotta trains for months after that. In those days, there was personality in it. There was respect and comradeship and gratitude in it. Today, it's all cut and dried, and there's no chance for bringing friendship to bear – or personality. You see what I mean? They don't know me anymore."

Success is an indifferent god, Willy learns. For, if that is all you wish to serve in life, that god will inevitably fail you. Yet, Willy persists in believing in the god success; this is what he tries to teach his sons. "Be liked," he says, "and you will never want ... personality always wins the day."

Throughout the play, there is the anguished cry against a system that dehumanizes people. When Willy is begging his young employer, Howard, to put him in the New York office, where he will not have to travel; he demeans himself miserably before this heartless young man, and cries out:

"I put 34 years into this firm, Howard, and now I can't pay the insurance! You can't eat the orange and throw the peel away – a man is not a piece of fruit!"

And earlier, Linda is defending Willy to his sons, particularly to Biff, who sees through his father's pretensions. She says passionately, in what is probably the greatest speech in the play:

"I don't say he's a great man. Willy Loman never made a lot of money. His name was never in the paper. He's not the finest character who ever lived. But he's a human being, and a terrible thing is happening to him. So attention must be paid. He's not to be allowed to fall into his grave like an old dog. Attention, attention must be finally paid to such a person. Attention must be paid."

But – we ask ourselves – in view of the inhumanity to persons in this world – is attention ever really paid?

The pressures drive Willy mad. He tries to plant a garden in the middle of the night by flashlight. Finally, he takes the car and drives over the side of the road, a suicide. He thinks he is doing the best thing that he can do. For now, at least, his family will have the insurance money.

But, at the grave, through her sobs, Linda cries: "Willy, I made the last payment on the house today. Today, dear. And there'll be nobody home."

And there it ends – the tragedy of Willy Loman.

What can we say in the face of such a drama? Well, surely I hope, not that chirpy sentimentality which, so often, we hear from our pulpits. As if somewhere there is a neat, religious, pious formula that will answer the problems of the Willy Lomans of this world. Or, that will magically straighten out the tragic dimensions of Willy Loman, which is somehow in all of us.

Tragedy does not resolve itself that easily. At some deep level in life, each one of us is wounded – no matter our age. We all struggle with principalities and powers, which seem sometimes greater than ourselves. We all surrender to the easy promise of some false god, which is always unable to deliver what it seemed to promise. We are anxious in life; and then somehow, we feel guilty about being anxious. We wear masks of equanimity and poise, concealing feelings of insecurity. And then we judge ourselves harshly for feeling what we actually feel.

No one of us, who faces life's profound ironies, ambiguities and wounds, dares scorn Willy Loman. Or condemn his inner struggle. For we could ask, too, when will the axe fall on us?

Aristotle's pity and fear. Those, too, are the appropriate responses to human tragedy. Pity at undeserved misfortune; fear that it could happen to one like myself.

There are no easy packaged answers. But there are certain glimpses and sounds, which speak of resources available to those who, however falteringly, place their trust in Jesus Christ.

One is to know that God accepts us as we are. Not as we might like to be, but as we really are. He comes to us not as some stern moral demand (which would only intensify our fears and insecurities) but as a person. A person who loves infinitely, richly, gladly. Who seeks those, who are aware that we do not have it made, do not have it together. Those who, in short, are deeply aware of our own humanity.

This loving leads to suffering. But in the face of human tragedy, only a suffering God will ever do. In Jesus of Nazareth, God accepts us as we are. Coming among us as a person who, too, bears our anxieties, temptations, passions, grandeur and misery -- all for the purpose of claiming us with liberating, undying love.

Biff says of his father, Willy: "He never knew who he was ..."

Some of us can say that about ourselves too – we do not know who we are.

But that does not shut us off from the love of God; from his acceptance of us as we are, in whatever confusion or muddle we walk. If we can glimpse that love, however dimly, perhaps with nothing more than an aching longing; then there opens for us new possibilities, new beginnings, and new life out of old graves.

And then, we discover another resource, too. Something, which is a bit precious in this day of self-centeredness and self-preoccupation: the quality of care for other human beings.

We hear in a new way Linda's anguished cry; "Attention, attention must be paid to such a person." That is, no person is beyond or unworthy of our care.

Whatever inevitable judgments we form must always be tempered by an attitude of ultimate mercy. Thus, whenever you hear -- inconceivably it seems to me -- certain Christians writing off other human beings as being unworthy. As being beyond concern and care, because they are of different ideologies or religions or mores. Or because they fail to meet the accepted images for behavior, go carefully there. Remember something else.

Remember that we are all in need. And that we are all claimed by God's love; a love so tenacious that it became wounded for us. And shows us that it is only the wounded, who can ever help one another. Reaffirm one another in our common humanity, our common plight.

And therefore, if we can help the Willy Lomans of the world, we should do it. If we can change the system under which they are beaten down and trod under foot, we should do it.

For this is what God – wounded for us – in his love beckons us to do. And when we respond, we find strange and wonderful things happen to us, too.

Prayer: Let me remember that I am loved as I am.

Amen

FAITH & LAUGHTER

"If you can't laugh in Heaven," Martin Luther once said, "then I don't want to go there."

That's good to remember. Because so often people seem to feel that to be religious, they must be somber and even dour.

The late Phyllis McGinley, marvelous poet of wit and grace, once put such a response in resigned perspective in her poem, "Sonnet from Assisi."

> Blind Francis, waiting to welcome Sister Death …
> Had heart for tune. With what remained of breath
> …
> Small-souled Elias gave him sermons and advice
> Instead of song; which simply proves once more
> What things are sure this side of paradise:
>
> Death, taxes and the counsel of the bore
> Though we outwit the tithe, make death our friend,
> Bores we have with us, even to the end.

Now faith is that risky kind of trust which affirms that the mystery of life is good. That mystery that remains always mysterious because we live in a world in which God can neither be proved nor evaded. Faith is not boring.

Faith, indeed, has about it a kind of lightness, a kind of nonchalance, a kind of letting-go quality. It is not far from laughter; the laughter of delight and surprise, which no one ever teaches a child. But which the child has, nonetheless.

It's a theme, which runs throughout the Bible. On the first day, so one writer has it, "the morning stars stand together an echo of laughter in creation."

Now, human laughter has many forms – the laughter, which springs from seeing human absurdities. The laughter, which is always appropriate, whenever we pretend to be more or less than human.

Pity the poor people who cannot laugh, somehow, at their own absurd moments, at their own awkwardness. That is the redemptive kind of humor, the kind of laughter, which can help heal.

Intriguingly enough, Norman Cousins -- American political journalist, author and professor -- lectured on the therapeutic value of laughter. In his true story, he told of being confined with a painful condition in a hospital. He finally checked out and went to a first-rate hotel -- it was cheaper. Watching old Marx Brothers and Charlie Chaplin films and Candid Camera reruns and taking vitamin therapy, he laughed himself well.

But human laughter can take other forms, too. The feverish laugher of escape from selfhood; the laughter of fools, which the writer of Ecclesiastes 7:16 describes as "the crackling of thorns under a pot."

Or it can be demonic laugher – from the sophisticated, even brilliant put-down of other people, to the racist stereotyping of others, to the sadistic glee of a Hitler watching films of garroted enemies.

However, the laughter, which is rooted in faith, is always lit by the spark of grace. It celebrates the unforeseeable.

The unforeseeable ways of God are shown forth in whom God chose to be His holy people. Of all the peoples in the world, God chose the Jews.

And the comedy breaks through as God tells them that he will be their God and they shall be His people. And He scarcely gets the words out, before they are dancing around some golden calf and carrying on with every agricultural deity and fertility god that they could find.

God's laugher is God's yes to overcoming the gloom of man's rejection.

Frederick Buechner, writer, theologian and ordained Presbyterian minister, in his little book, *Telling the Truth*, describes the gospel as tragedy and comedy and fairy tale – three literary categories. He is writing about election – about the unforeseen goodness of God in seeking people.

"The gospel as comedy," he writes, "is the coming together of Mutt and Jeff, the Captain and the Kids, the Wizard of Oz and the Scarecrow. Man in his unending littleness, prepared for the worst but rarely for the best; prepared for the possible, but rarely for the impossible."

God's good news breaks into a world, where the news has been so bad for so long that when it is good, nobody hears it much, except for a few. And who are the few who hear it?

They are the ones, who labor and are heavy-laden like everybody else. But who, unlike everybody else, know that they labor and are heavy-laden. They are the last people you might expect to hear it. Themselves, the bad jokes and stooges and scarecrows of the world, the tax collectors and whores and misfits. They are the poor people, the broken people, the ones, who in terms of the world's wisdom, are children and madmen and fools. And who of us isn't?

Rich or poor, successes or failures, as the world counts it; they are the ones who are willing to believe in miracles. Because they know it will take a miracle to fill the empty place inside them, where grace and peace belong, with grace and peace.

Having used up all their tears, they have nothing but laughter left. Maybe the truth of God is that it's too good not to be true.

Prayer: Let me laugh at and with myself ... all the way to Heaven.

Amen

FATALISM & FAITH

"All things work together for good to them that love God, to them who are called according to his purpose," we learn in Romans 8:28. The Apostle Paul was speaking about what we often call the providence of God. But how shall we think about that in the face of human suffering?

In 1902, on the small Caribbean island of Martinique, Mount Pelée – a volcano, which had been dormant for centuries – suddenly erupted and spewed a deadly mass of lava and hot ashes upon the city of St. Pierre, which lies at the foot of the mountain. It all happened so quickly that no one could escape. Nearly thirty thousand persons died that day in St. Pierre. saints and sinners, old people and little children. Only one person survived – a man by the name of Auguste Ciparis, who was a criminal and in jail. Was this God's providence?

How do we confront this – as we all confront human suffering, the incoherence and incongruity of life? None of us is exempt. Whether we are pious or impious, we all confront a checkered existence. Is it chance? Fate? God's will?

Different responses, of course, are given. The agnostic or atheist will say there is nothing behind such happenings, except pure chance; good luck for one, bad luck for another. Other people hold a kind of cosmic concept of a pre-determined destiny and fate for each person.

The ancient Greeks expressed this belief in their myth of the three goddesses, who spin, gather and cut the thread of each human life. Some of the great religions of the world hold to this fatalistic view of life.

But it is not a Christian view. For, if it were; then human beings would be simply like leaves, blown by implacable winds of fate. And there would be no meaning to such words as freedom, morality, right, wrong, sin or forgiveness.

No. Christian faith affirms creation as essentially purposeful. There is a coherency in life, in nature; there is order and predictability. But these forces operate without regard for human worthiness or unworthiness. Jesus stated God's intentions clearly in Matthew 5:45 saying: "He maketh his sun to rise on the evil and the good, and sendeth rain on the just and the unjust."

Fire warms the scoundrel, as it warms the saint; cancer strikes the body of a much-needed mother or father, as well as the body of a wanton playboy. It is possible to say that we cannot possibly believe in God when we confront the enormity of suffering people in this world.

But as Catholic priest and theologian, Hans Küng asks,

"Can this not be reversed? It is only if there is a God that we can look at all this immense suffering in the world. It is only in trusting faith in the incomprehensible, always greater God; that man can stride in justifiable hope through that broad, deep river. Conscious of the fact that a hand is stretched out to us across the dark gulf of suffering and evil."

Jesus never explained suffering. Rather, he endured it. Even though innocent in the sight of God – endured it. Not like Job, fictionally – but in reality. Thirsting, and inch-by-inch, dying on a cross, crying out toward the end as we read in Mark 15:35, "My God, my God, why hast Thou forsaken me?"

And while he was hanging there, with God publicly absent; nonetheless, there was a hidden divine presence. And this is a clue for us. Even manifestly senseless suffering and death can yet <u>have</u> a meaning, can <u>acquire</u> a meaning.

It is always a hidden meaning. And not one, which we can manufacture. But accept, in the light of the suffering and dying of Jesus.

It is not a meaning given automatically. There is no wishful thinking here, no glorification of suffering proclaimed, no cheap and easy consolation. But a meaning is nonetheless offered – which can be freely accepted. One has to decide.

A person can reject this hidden meaning – in spite, or bitterness, or cynicism and despair. Or we can also accept it – in believing trust in Him, who endured the senseless suffering and death of Jesus with meaning. Then, rebellion or frustration can be let go.

For the God, whom Jesus reveals is not only the God of the strong, the healthy, the successful. He is rather one, who takes upon himself our burden – and becomes the Father of the Lost. The hidden one who pursues us through our history, even in the darkness and futility of it; mercifully sustaining us, even in our remoteness from Him.

God's love does not protect us <u>from</u> all suffering. But it protects us <u>in</u> all suffering. When we experience this, then we can understand the words: that in everything, God works for good to those who love Him (by responding to his searching love.)

Then, tentatively, we can see strange meaning woven in the midst of suffering. Lebanese-American poet, and philosopher *Kahlil Gibran* writes about Pain:

"Your pain is the breaking of the shell that encloses your understanding.

"Even as the stone of the fruit must break, that its heart may stand in the sun, so must you know pain …

"Much of your pain is self-chosen.

"It is the bitter potion by which the physician within you heals your sick self.

"Therefore trust the physician, and drink his remedy in silence and tranquility:

"For his hand, though heavy and hard, is guided by the tender hand of the Unseen,

"And the cup He brings, though it burn your lips, has been fashioned of the clay which the Potter has moistened with His own sacred tears."

And from his words on Joy & Sorrow …

"The deeper that sorrow carves into your being, the more joy you can contain."

Here a little 5-year-old girl, who after a serious illness, was found to have lost her sight, her hearing, her speech. What goodness was there? But years later – as an old woman—she stood in Harvard Yard and moved cynics to tears; with her simple testimony to the hidden meaning of God's grace in her suffering.

She, of course, was Helen Keller – from whom others received strength, hope and courage to bear their own obscure and un-noticed suffering.

But, we are not alone. For even at the moment when everything goes wrong for us; there is One who, nonetheless, still searches for us. Still bids us to know Him more deeply. Seeks us at a level deeper than ordinary pleasures and helps prepare us for the greater life that is to come.

Prayer: "I believe, help my unbelief."

Amen

FEELING GUILTY

There's something that troubles every one of us – the problem of guilt. And yet, guilt is such a complex phenomenon as to almost defy description. Any attempt to define guilt precisely is rather like an attempt to define light. We all experience light and can recognize it, but who among us can precisely explain it?

Sigmund Freud, the father of modern psychiatry, pointed out that guilt is the inevitable consequence of all civilization. Any society – no mater how primitive – requires some restraint, some inhibitions, some "no-nos." Without them, social structure and relationships would be impossible.

In this sense, there is really almost something positive to be said about guilt. If you think that's shocking, think for a moment about the absence of guilt.

Think of the youthful gang of young men in Stanley Kubrick's film, *Clockwork Orange*, who get their kicks, their sense of stimulation by beating, killing, and maiming random victims.

What's missing there? Well, a sense of guilt. They have no internalized sense of restraint, they lack any sense of loyalty to anyone – ultimately, even to themselves.

You see, just as physical pain is a kind of sentinel for physical health, which warns of possible threats to your body, so – in some sense, guilt is a kind of warning system, too. And it's absolutely necessary for social relationships and spiritual growth.

To try to define the indefinable, then: guilt is that special form of anxiety, which reminds us of our essential relationship to others. It warns us against that which threatens life, that which regresses to what is inhuman and destructive. It is a growing pain that separates human beings from beasts.

In the late Peabody Award-winning journalist, Eric Sevareid's moving autobiography, *Not So Wild A Dream,* he tells of a civilian plane crash on a flight between Burma and China in World War II. All of the passengers survived – except one. They found his body under the wreckage. And Sevareid stood there thinking:

"If there had not been two or three of us trying to get out when the crew arrived at the door, the few seconds saved would perhaps have meant the saving of his life. One could, if he wished, move the point of responsibility further back. If there had been definite orders for and organization of the passengers – all of them amateurs. If the passengers had been briefed on the ground. If the C-45 had not been used for passengers in the first place. If Washington had not ordered these planes to The Hump run before they were perfected …. There was a long chain of errors and happenstance, and no one could determine that this or that was the fatal link."

What is this objective journalist expressing here? Well, something more that mere remorse. Rather a sense of guilt, a sense of participation in the whole human process, a sense of ownership in death and tragedy.

It's like the brakes on a car – necessary for us to control and manage the enormous power of drives and passions. But, how quickly this kind of sensitivity and necessary awareness gets twisted around. Then, a false sense of guilt emerges – which sucks away our power and can even destroy us!

The real problem for most of us neurotics is this: we just keep driving the car with our foot on the brake of guilt all the time. And so, we diminish the power, which is available from our own instinctual nature.

We feel guilty if we haven't measured up to society's criteria for success. One of the crises of middle years in reckoning and calculating just how far we've gotten up the status ladder and how far we still have to go.

And we feel guilty when we fail to meet our own inner expectations:

We are

- angry when we want to see ourselves as gentle.
  or
- impatient when we want to be understanding.
  or
- callous and indifferent when we want to be sensitive.
  or
- critical when we want to be accepting.
  or
- busy when we want to be caring.

We fail to be the person we, at some level, want to be – or believe we were meant to be. And we feel guilty.

And guilt can leave us feeling chronically exhausted. It can invade our dreams and leave us fatigued. It can fuel a sense of depression and rob us of self-esteem and hope. It can rob us, too, of feelings and passion.

There are lots of strategies to employ for dealing with this kind of disabling guilt. Among them …

Blame other people: The Peanuts cartoon character, Charlie Brown stands over a broken lamp and mourns: "If I can't blame society, who can I blame?"

Or pretend it doesn't exist. Repress it.

The trouble with these strategies – including the sophisticated argument for society to lower its constraints and expectations, in order to induce less guilt – is that they just don't work.

Repressed guilt just ticks away like a time bomb, with the potential to explode at some time – bringing harm to ourselves and others.

What to do, then?

Christianity is ultimately not doctrines, not dogmas – but Jesus Christ.

And in Jesus Christ, God deals with our inevitable burden of guilt. Our guilt, then, becomes the stuff for redemption itself.

At the heart of the Christian message is good news; you are counted as a child of God. You are accepted, regarded by God himself as an object of inestimable value. Not for your actions -- or your inactions. But rather from the mysterious and gracious act of God.

Whatever there is within us that is tragically flawed and not as it should be. Whatever "bad-mouthing" we do to ourselves, our mutual hope and Christian commitment is that there is no rejection.

A rebuke, repentance, restitution – as best we can – yes.

But rejection – no. Never. Your guilt – and mine – is not the mark of ultimate rejection. There is no ultimate rejection. There is rather, incredibly, ultimate love.

God's "yes" overcomes even the "no" we lay upon ourselves and others. He looks at us as worthy.

Christianity is not a religion of control, but a religion of redemption. We can admit our guilt. Not deny it. Nor repress it. Christians do not need to find ourselves caught in the abrasive and frustrating web of repression, of shoulds and oughts, and control.

No one can speak the word forgiveness – except in the name of God.

To deal with our guilt, we need more than mere techniques. A psychiatrist can help us uncover hidden fears or deep-seated guilt, but as David Stafford Clark, a British psychiatrist and author, writes:

"Thrown back upon himself, the patient finds no solace, nor comfort. He looks to his psychiatrist. He cannot get power from him or her. If he could, it would not be maintained for life."

Then, Dr. Clark adds:

"Where then can a person turn? As a psychiatrist, I know of no answer to this question. As a man, I can only say with humility, 'I believe in God.'"

We all punish ourselves with guilt.

But be of good courage. There is one, even Jesus Christ, who has taken our burden into himself – and gives us back hope and release and space enough to be ourselves. And that is good news indeed!

Prayer: There, but for the grace of God, go I. Let me turn from my guilt, and live!

Amen

FINDING HAPPINESS

In every one of us there is no stronger drive than the desire for happiness.

Very often, when I meet with a young couple for pre-marital counseling and ask them: "What do you really want from this marriage? What is it that you are really seeking and expecting? The response will be, 'happiness.'"

Everyone wants to be happy.

And we Americans are the only people in the world to have declared our independence as a nation by stating – in Jefferson's famous words – that we have an inalienable right, a right which no one can take away: to life, liberty and the pursuit of happiness.

But just what is this happiness we pursue – and where is it to be found? Well, these are questions as old as humanity.

If you Google it, you'll find a host of definitions: pleasure, contentment, satisfaction, cheerfulness, merriment, gaiety, joy, joyfulness, glee, delight, good spirits, lightheartedness, well-being, enjoyment.

If you read the comic strip, *Peanuts,* you'll find Lucy hugging a startled Snoopy under the caption: "Happiness is a warm puppy!"

If you ask folks at a singles bar, they might say, "Happiness is a dry martini."

So, there is no universal agreement as to what precisely constitutes this happiness we all hunger for.

Yet strangely enough, even though we can't adequately define it, we've all experienced it.

We know when we're happy and when we're not. We know that it isn't constant – it isn't something we can hold onto for long periods.

Dr. Faust. who in Goethe's famous tale sells his soul to the Devil for a moment of sublime happiness, speaks for all of us:

"And so from longing to delight I reel

And even in delight, I pine for longing."

So, happiness – whatever it is – is elusive. Yet, how willing someone is to come along and tell us where to find it.

American actress and writer Joanna Barnes, spoke of her childhood when: "Books and movies told me what would make me happy. Jane got the puppy that Mother and Daddy said they couldn't afford. And the four of them lived happily ever after. No mention of paper-training responsibilities, worming, distemper or biting your best friend.

"But the dog I had as a kid became ill and had to be put away ... and the one that followed was stolen."

Or, we're told that in our middle years, money and success will guarantee happiness.

Yet, we know from glimpses into the lives of people endowed with these very things that there is often terrible pain, isolation and fear. Someone still delivers roses to the grave of Marilyn Monroe, who died tragically despite her possession of wealth, fame and beauty.

Or, in the older years – the so-called Golden Years, we're told that leisure time will now bring happiness. When, in truth, older people in our society are often callously treated as if they are useless and have nothing to contribute. Nothing significant to do with their time.

Happiness, then, isn't something, which can be drunk, purchased or commanded from the abundance of possessions, status or time. Indeed, happiness isn't something we can really get directly.

What then is a clue to finding it? In the gospel, which Jesus proclaimed, the message is very simple. The person who is ready to lose his life, truly finds it. And the person who strives to save his life, to lay hold of happiness without really letting go of himself, is the one who can't find life at all.

And that speaks very directly to the drive for happiness, too.

Happiness is really a by-product of being absorbed in something worthwhile, something outside yourself.

It flows from an active, engaged life; it flows from purposeful service with and to others.

Happiness is serendipity. That's a beautiful old word, which means that you sometimes find something very valuable while you're looking for something else

It may seem old fashioned. Our society is enthralled by the idea of instant and immediate gratification. The idea of sacrificing something of yourself, investing something of yourself in some personal way for someone outside of yourself, runs counter to the present cultural stream.

But the truth, which Jesus enunciated, is still verified by human experience. You know it yourself. You know that happiness isn't something you can contrive; it isn't really something self-conscious (conscious of self) at all.

It comes rather when you're engaged beyond yourself. That moment comes – a moment that springs from caring and commitment and giving.

And it passes – for no one can live at "peak moments" all the time. New tasks beckon. New goals present themselves. And happiness returns, as a person recommits him or herself to the challenges and opportunities in life.

So, Thomas Jefferson wisely spoke of the process ... the pursuit of happiness. Because it is dynamic; it surprises us as we lose ourselves in service.

And it can come to people in the most deprived circumstances, in situations, which the shallow and selfish among us could never imagine.

In my first parish, I knew a teenage boy, who had been afflicted from birth with a terrible spastic condition. He was not always mobile. He had difficulty speaking at times. He didn't have control over his limbs or movements.

He went through some hard-to-imagine experiences – the loneliness of adolescence was compounded a hundred-fold for him.

But Bobby had a mind and he had courage. Gradually, he came to accept his great limitations. He worked hard not to let them defeat him. He set himself toward some modest goals, which he could realize. And in his pursuit, involving other people in working towards them, he discovered profound moments of happiness.

He could contribute something to others. And I'll never forget his face when he told me: "I'm so happy."

Blind, deaf, mute Helen Keller said:

"I can see and this is why I can be so happy in what you call the dark. But which, to me, is golden. I can see a God-made world, not a man-made world."

You've heard the familiar words of Jesus in Matthew 5:7, from the Sermon on the Mount, the Beatitudes. "Blessed are the poor in spirit, for theirs is the kingdom of Heaven ... blessed are the merciful."

In the original language, the word "blessed" was translated: How happy!

Now, listen again: How happy are those who know they are spiritually in need ....

Those, in short, who know that they cannot really fulfill themselves – that they need other people beyond themselves to be themselves. That they need and hunger for a relationship with the Creator, if they are to be fully human.

In a catechism from the Reformation, the question is simply put: What is the chief end of Man and, presumably, Woman?

And the happy and comprehensive answer is: to glorify God and enjoy Him forever. Glorifying God by giving of our best self, we find ourselves and are found by Him.

Prayer: Grant me the serendipity of happiness as I strive to glorify Thee.

Amen

FORGIVENESS

A truck driver stopped at a roadside diner. He was seated at a table eating his dinner; when four rough, tough motorcyclists roared up, came in, looked around, walked over to the truck driver's table and said:

"We want this table … take off."

The trucker said,

"But, I'm not finished."

One of the cyclists picked up a water glass, poured it over the trucker's dinner and said:

"Now you are, go!"

The trucker put his money on the table, picked up his baseball cap and walked out. The four cyclists laughed it up for a few minutes. And the one who'd poured the water said:

"He wasn't much of a man, was he?"

The waitress, who was two tables away and had a clear view of the parking lot, overheard him and said:

"He's not much of a truck driver either. He just ran over four motorcycles."

Sweet revenge. Few feelings have been so classically celebrated. Vengeance is the dominant passion in Herman Melville's Moby Dick. And Shakespeare's Hamlet is a tragedy of revenge. The young prince spends his life avenging his father's death. "The time is out of joint," he cried. "O cursed spite, that ever I was born to set it right."

Vengeance is as up to date as this morning's newspaper – whether among Isis terrorists or the violent gangs on their turfs on the streets of America. We all know its power. The urge to "get even" is a perennial temptation: "Don't get mad, get even," modern folk wisdom advises. Who doesn't know the desire to settle scores, to take things into one's own hands?

But Christians are called to a style of life, which is free of vengeance. And this counsel contains deep wisdom.

Consider, first of all, that vengeance is destructive, even harmful. And harmful not only to the one who is its target, but also the one who delivers it. A person, consumed by the impulse for vengeance, is robbed of a sense of inner-harmony. In its place comes a disorganizing anxiety, which disrupts dreams and sours relationships.

Vengeance stops prayer, misdirects energy, can rob the middle years of their creativity and crown old age with thorns of bitterness. And further, vengeance is ultimately futile. Evil is not – and never has been – the answer to evil. Vengeance simply perpetuates the dreary cycle of sin/retribution, sin/retribution – tearing and rending the fabric of human life.

But most importantly, the reason why vengeance is wrong is because something else is right. That something is forgiveness.

In the Lord's Prayer, we pray: "Forgive us our debts or trespasses, as we forgive our debtors or those who trespass against us." And this petition does not indicate some sort of quid pro quo – that God only forgives as we forgive. No. It does mean that if we aren't open to forgive another – then we aren't open to receive forgiveness, ourselves.

Jesus preached, "I say to you, love your enemies and pray for those who persecute you ...."

In 1984, Harvard psychiatrist and Pulitzer Prize winner for his books on children and change, Robert Coles stated that what children need, as much as food, clothing and a good education, is moral purpose. It is clear, he said, that living in affluent circumstances does not guarantee a rewarding spiritual life.

As a matter of fact, he reported, the best teacher he ever had on moral education was a 6-year-old girl, whose parents were poor, hard-working, long-suffering, illiterate Black people in New Orleans. Ruby, the 6-year-old, was one of four Black children who pioneered desegregation in two New Orleans elementary schools in 1960. Every day, she and another girl had to be escorted to school by federal marshals, facing crowds who shouted that they would kill them and who called them every vile name there was.

As a psychiatrist, Dr. Coles (who had been trained to study what happens to children under stress) wanted to find out what would happen to Ruby's psychological development. The teacher admitted that she couldn't understand how Ruby could take it. "She experiences this every day and yet, seems so composed," the teacher said. "She is so eager to learn and is such a nice child."

Dr. Coles was puzzled, too. When they thought they observed Ruby talking to some of the people haranguing her, he asked her about it.

It turned out that Ruby was praying for her tormentors. When Dr. Coles asked Ruby why she was praying, Ruby replied, "because my parents, minister and grandmother said I should."

"Do you think it will do any good?" she was asked. Her response: "We must pray for them even if it doesn't do any good." But admitted she prayed even when she didn't feel much like it. She prayed, because she knew the example of Jesus who prayed for his tormentors from the cross, "Father, forgive them, for they know not what they do."

That – said Coles – was her moral education, noting that people come to develop some of the most admirable qualities in response to pain, suffering and hardship.

But if we left it at that, then, I don't think any of us would find much true comfort or hope. For we know, that our lives are riddled by anxieties and self concerns. And that it is from these that the perversions of our hearts – including the impulse for vengeance – flow.

But the One, who suffered on the cross, is more than a role model for us. He is a source of power, too. He can enable us to receive forgiveness for our own sins; for our own impulses toward hatred of others.

And in that process, at that sacred place, we can receive the power to grow somewhat, to be nudged by the spirit in the direction of a more Christ-like life.

Prayer: Give me the peace and inner-harmony, which surpasses all human understanding in the power to bless my enemies.

Amen

FREEDOM & RESPONSIBILITY

In many ways, life is a matter of emphasis. It is shaped by where you put the stress, by what you emphasize. In placing emphasis, we often fall off on one extreme or the other.

We emphasize one dimension of experience so strongly that we neglect the corresponding reality. Thus, we become strong on this – and weak on that.

Charles Darwin, best known for his theories of evolution, mourned that everything else in life atrophied, because he had to pursue – with single-minded devotion – only this one scientific aspect.

Or, we all know people who are so set on being honest that they become indifferent about the feelings of others. They simply blurt out the truth to the hurt of others and then, defend their behavior by saying: "Well, at least I'm honest."

Others are at the other extreme – so committed to not offending anyone that they never express themselves. Perhaps, living with the hope that when they die, someone will think to say: "I never heard her say anything bad about anyone." Of course, no one will ever know how she felt about anything, either.

Now, none of us can do everything. You can only be you – as redundant as that may sound. You simply cannot be strong or balanced or competent in every area.

Nor, are we called to be. Christians are delivered from the curse of perfectionism. In a letter found in John 2:1, the Apostle John wrote, "My little children, these things write I unto you, that ye sin not. And if any man sin, we have an advocate with the Father, Jesus Christ the righteous," who intercedes for us.

We are never going to have it all together, have it made, be without troubles or failings; no. But, on the other hand, precisely because we have been touched by the love of God, we are free to grow, to develop in a more holistic way, our own potential.

Or, as John again puts it, we are free to walk in the same way in which Jesus walked.

But what does that mean? I think that it means our journey through life is one, which encompasses both freedom and responsibility.

By now, most of us have grown tired of living up to other people's expectations. Teenagers tire of living up to parent's expectations, and parents tire of living up to their children's expectations.

Some people get so tired, they rebel, and the rebellion is sometimes so angry that they concentrate on living contrary to the expectations they reject. Many who don't rebel, nonetheless, fantasize about rebelling; where we can shuck certain expectations and be free from duty.

You may remember some years ago, a Manhattan bus driver, having had his fill of routine and regulations, started driving one morning and didn't stop until he got to Miami, Florida. Bus driver AWOL.

Two weeks later, when he returned to New York City, a cheering crowd of people met him with acclamation. He had become a hero by doing something that many would like to have done – just to break loose, and be done with the whole business.

On the other hand, we are paying the price for living by our impulses, doing what we want, when we want. And we're going to be paying on this one for years to come. Hedonism – living that is dictated only by our pleasure and our pain – is not only destructive. It is empty. Its promise is like a mirage in the desert. Doing what you want when you want is a subtle, and all the more devastating bondage.

Doing your own thing, without regard for God and everyone else, not only rides roughshod over others; it rides roughshod over your own highest self.

Now, few of us are blatant hedonists – valuing everything only by our own pain or pleasure. Yet, all of us struggle with temptation to find a comfortable place, where we can avoid the needs and hurts of others.

And something happens: what about those who once were idealists, committed to changing the world and moving history a little nudge toward the Kingdom? What happened to their dreams and commitment – those who now say: "We just want to be happy!"

What happened to the neighbor who was so given to the biblical command found in Matthew 22:39: "…thou shalt love thy neighbour as thyself." He once made himself available, but now has withdrawn to his own little corner of the street?

What happened to the modest souls who once, in their own way, were trying to make the world a bit better and brighter. But have exchanged their outlook for a good case of skepticism about any and all efforts?

For one thing, we are afflicted with the "nothing can be done" disease, of which former White House press secretary and political commentator, Bill Moyers has written: "Depleted of energy and bereft of hope, we conclude. 'Oh, what's the use!'

"With life so out of control, we lose any sense of power and forsake the conviction that our behavior and attitudes count for anything. Accompanying the feeling of powerlessness is the defensive attitude of: 'If I don't take care of myself, no one else will.'

"So we've come full cycle from the self-centeredness of infancy through the idealism of youth. And the creativity of adulthood back to the self-centeredness of retreat to old age – "me, myself, and I." Or at most, to the attitude of 'me, my wife, my son John and his wife – us four and no more.'"

Moyers confesses: "I vacillate, as I suspect you do, between determination to change society and the desire to retreat into the snuggeries of myself and my family."

That's a condition common to all of us … we are, after all, participants in our own historical situation; we are affected by the strong currents of the me decades. But surely, something in our faith prevents us from being comfortable with this emphasis.

Freedom and responsibility. How do we find balance? Here, as always, we find the clues in Jesus of Nazareth. He is the model for authentic freedom and responsibility.

Never was there one more truly free to be His own man – free from the pressure of public opinion, free from seduction by an easy out, free from the self-protecting urgings of family and friends. He would not be intimidated, not even by those who held in their hands the power of His life and death.

In the Book of John 19:10, it is written that Pontius Pilate panicked and asked a silent Jesus, "Speakest thou not unto me? Knowest thou not that I have power to crucify thee, and have power to release thee?"

Steadily, Jesus answered that Pilate had no power over Him unless it had been given from above ....

Jesus would not be intimidated, manipulated, coerced, compelled, bought or bribed.

In John 10:17-18, Jesus told Pilate, "I lay down my life, ... no man taketh it from me, but I lay it down of myself. I have power to lay it down, and I have power to take it again. This commandment have I received from my Father."

And so have we received the charge to live and die as free human beings. That freedom is given. It cannot be taken from us. We lose it only when we surrender it. The ultimate freedom of a human being is the freedom to live and die as he or she will. Everything else can be taken away, but not the freedom to choose the purpose, principles and perspectives, by which we will each do our living and our dying.

Authentic freedom is choosing to give yourself to that which is worth the gift of yourself. The truly and fully free Jesus chose to lay down his life on behalf of others. In exercising that response-ability was the fulfillment of His freedom.

Prayer: Let me choose to give myself to that which is worthy of the gifts you have given me.

Amen

GOD'S LOVE

What power can give us the strength, which we need for the turbulent, violent and chaotic waters of nature and our time? God's love.

Only what the world so quickly dismisses as fragile and powerless: the power of unconditional love. A love, which identifies, which goes to the depths, which accepts, which enhances; rather than manipulates. A love, which never acts coercively. But rather creates situations in which out of our own free will, we want to respond. To become what it is that love wants us to be.

Now, we catch glimpses of this Christ-like love even in our own terrible times. In the epic film, Ghandi is a middle-class, English-trained lawyer. He comes to realize that only through the path of complete identification could anyone begin to rouse the great masses of people in India to solidarity and liberation.

There is a scene in the film where young Ghandi addresses the rich and powerful members of the Congress Party. Most are quite bored with his appearance. Some get up to leave. But soon, they are listening. For he tells them, as they lie on their soft carpets, that what they are saying and what they are doing is quite irrelevant. Utterly meaningless to the great majority of poverty-ridden people. And only if they come to understand the basic needs and aspiration of the masses, can they ever find the pathway to the freedom they crave.

So, Gandhi goes to live as modestly and humbly as any village peasant. And when others were tempted to violence, he refused. And took into his own body the pain of fasting, until violence was stopped and a strategy of respect was adopted.

The suffering servant. Not many years later, a young Christian in America was to choose the same strategy of suffering love and non-violence for the cause of justice and equal treatment. Martin Luther King, Jr. wrote from prison: "We shall match your capacity to inflict suffering by our capacity to endure suffering. Be assured that we will wear you down by our capacity to suffer. One day, we shall win freedom, but not only for ourselves. We shall so appeal to your heart and conscience that we shall win you in the process and our victory will be a double victory."

Fifty years after he was gunned down, his 9-year-old granddaughter would mirror his words in a peaceful 2018 March for Our Lives demonstration against gun violence in Washington DC. "My grandfather had a dream that his four little children would not be judged by the color of their skin, but by the content of their character," she said, referencing her grandfather's famous speech.

"I have a dream that enough is enough. That this should be a gun-free world. Period."

As she delivered her speech not far from where her grandfather gave his famous address, the crowd of hundreds of thousands of children, teenagers and parents roared their approval. But, Ms. King wasn't finished. She then, led the chant: 'Spread the word. Have you heard? All across the nation. We … are going to be. A great generation.'"

Now, this is always fragile and risky in our kind of world, where people are accustomed to external force.

Because God's love is un-manipulative. Because He treasures our freedom. If, above all, He wants us to love Him of our own free will, then we must be free to not love Him. Free, even to resist and reject His love. Free to deny it, as with the crucifixion of Christ and the assassinations of both Mahatma Gandhi and Martin Luther King.

That is the terrible burden of our terrifying and grand human freedom.

But Christians belong to the community of the servant, and we ourselves are to bear witness to the power of uncoercive love. Of love that gives for the sake of others in their need. Of love that goes above and beyond and keeps at it, despite the pain of rejection and hostility. It is the love, which was made manifest in Jesus, who did not remain aloof. But plunged into human life fully and deeply, in order to bring humankind new life and hope.

Prayer: Whatever Christ-like love I have learned or received or heard or seen in Him, let me put into practice in my own life.

Amen

GRATITUDE FOR THE ORDINARY

O all ye of tender heart
Forgiving others, take your part
O sing ye, Alleluia!
Ye, who long pain and sorrow bear
Praise God and on him, cast your care.

Wrote Francis of Assisi, paraphrasing the words of Saint Paul to rejoice always and give thanks in all circumstances.

In all circumstances – on good days and bad days – give thanks.

Both these saints, these great sensitive men of spirit, are really saying that praise and gratitude is our true, natural condition. And authentic response as human beings.

There's a small event in the life of Jesus, which speaks of our more perennial human reaction: ten lepers were healed, but only one came back to thank Jesus for having been made clean.

And I think that most of us would have to confess that genuine gratitude, true thankfulness, doesn't come easily for us. We are so often distracted – so caught up in our dreams or so lost in our own disappointments. So busy deferring for the future or rehearsing regrets of the past, that we readily lose all perspective.

We're so preoccupied with ourselves that we sometimes miss the very best things, which are already at hand, already there, already happening. We particularly forget that the real meaning of life lies in the ordinary quite common round of our daily experience.

Christianity insists that grace comes through the commonplace. That everyday people and everyday things become the means by which we are related to the depths of our existence, to the very love of God.

For it is in the ordinary everyday commonplace experiences of life that God meets us. That true meaning and real love are to be found. And that is why daily gratitude is truly right and appropriate.

Very few of us live at some peak of high adventure. Very few of us become famous or have monuments raised to our names.

We just go along, doing pretty much the same sort of things day after day. And so we easily forget that the day-to-day rhythm of life is the arena, in which the richest meaning is found.

We become human in the network of everyday. Where we believe in people, trust each other, love and give life to each other, try to do our best and leave things better than they were. It is love – not fame or popularity – that bridges the gaps of life and makes whole the lives of all of us.

Look at what it is that troubles and vexes us most. Philosophical questions? Metaphysical problems? No. It is the commonplace, the ordinary things that distract or bedevil us. The practical, ordinary things that we do or don't do that worry us.

It is our relationships with each other, which can enhance our lives. To be present to each other in really sharing life is a far greater accomplishment than almost anything else we can do.

Every now and then, we have occasion to say to someone else: "You made my day." Each of us has it in us to do that for the others of us – to make their days.

And what is life but today, tomorrow and the day after that?

The great causes and the larger purposes are played out a day at a time. And one ordinary day has a way of giving shape to other days. Any day may be the day when the fog of doubt and despair lifts; so you can see again. The smoke of some ruins clears enough for you to see beyond all the debris to the Eternal. For life to come back into focus for you, having been casual about your God-intended self, to come back to your senses and head for the Father's house.

And the facilitator, the enabler, for such a day is likely to be someone who is with you in your very ordinary, everyday life. Who hears you out, who may poke an elbow of reality and hope into your ribs. Who extends a helping hand, and even walks with you on your way.

Now others may miss the tag, which identifies the source for goodness of the everyday in life. But Christians will have no trouble in recognizing that God mediates his grace through ordinary events and ordinary people.

Others may not get it without some kind of label attached. But Christians will know that work – even drudgery – can sometimes bring God's own beatitudes. Or that fun, even hilarity, can be the very balm of God for us. Or that doctors can supply His mercy. Or that friends can furnish His graciousness. Or that family, best of all, can show us His love.

All of these everyday people, all of these commonplace actions can and do show us God's presence; even when we, the actors, may not know it ourselves.

It is the understanding, the forgiveness, the acceptance, the love of real people that is sacramental of the grace of God. In them – through them -- the grace of God makes itself real through the commonplace. Everyday things and everyday people become signs and seals of God's understanding, God's forgiveness, God's own love. Such is the depth of creation – and the depth of the Creator's love for us.

Thornton Wilder's play, *Our Town* is the story of a day-to-day life in a little New England town.

In one scene, after her death, Emily – the young girl – learns that if she wishes, she may return to life again. But is warned that it will not be an easy experience. "Choose an unimportant day. Choose the least important day in your life. It will be important enough," she is told.

So, she selects a happy and ordinary day – her twelfth birthday. The stage-manager/narrator cautions her: "You will not only re-live it, but you will watch yourself living it. And as you watch it, you will see the thing that they – down there – never know. You see the future. You know what's going to happen afterwards."

Despite the warning, Emily returns and speaks to her recreated past that cannot hear her, the past where people are going about their everyday tasks and commonplace routines.

"Oh, Mama," Emily cries, "just look at me one minute as though you really see me. Mama, fourteen years have gone by. I'm dead. You're a grandmother, Mama ...Wally's dead, too ... We felt just terrible about it ... Don't you remember?

"But just for a moment now we're all together. Mama, just for a moment, we're happy. Let's look at one another."

Let's look at one another; let's look with gratitude.

We can celebrate how much we share God's goodness in the love that makes us mean something to each other. We can recognize that in the ordinary, everyday, commonplace of life; God comes to us and seeks us and places his claim upon us, in love. And that the life of the Spirit is not lived in any place but the regular round of trying to love each other a little more.

Now, it may be that in the distraction of life – we lose sight of this. But even if we've glimpsed it – for just a moment -- we will have retained an essential perspective. Something, which will restore our spirits and help us value what God has already given each of us.

In the play, Emily mourns the fact that life is not appreciated by the living.

Emily: "Does anyone realize what life is, while they're living it? Every minute?"

Stage Manager and narrator: "No. Saints and poets maybe ... they do some."

Prayer: God, grant us eyes to see the goodness of your love around us, in the everyday, ordinary places where we live and move and have our being. Let us join all creatures, great and small, in gratitude for the gift of your presence.

Amen

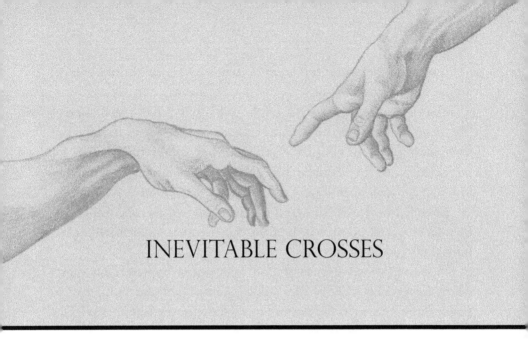

INEVITABLE CROSSES

What is life? Who is really capable of understanding the essence of human life? Of embracing all the complexities, the elusive qualities, the contradictions and ambiguities, which make up human existence?

Maybe that's why poets, artists, novelists and songwriters are able to portray, more adequately than others, the incredible mystery of human experience.

In the song that Frank Sinatra made famous, he sings:

"That's life, that's what people say
You're ridin' high in April
Shot down in May …

I've been a puppet, a pauper, a pirate
A poet, a pawn and a king …

And I know one thing.

Each time I find myself flat on my face,
I pick myself up and get back in the race.

Or as the French say, "C'est la vie." Such is life.

Life is essentially mysterious.

It seems to me that in this mysterious existence; two realities, at least, are encountered by all of us.

One is the fact of what we might call "the graciousness of being." The beauty, the coherence, the beneficence of life. We experience this sometimes when we encounter the surprising power for healing, for regeneration and for renewal in life. There is a kind of economy in things; in which apparently, nothing is ever wasted or entirely lost.

But side-by-side with this great positive mystery is a second reality. The mystery of a dark power which is not beneficent; but which strikes and hurts, kills and destroys.

In nature, we see it as a kind of capricious or unpredictable thing, which respects no form of life. Which seems blind and indifferent to personal consciousness – as when an earthquake strikes or a tornado levels. And in human nature, we see it tragically true, as well.

In his poem, *Prussian Nights*, Russian novelist and historian, Aleksandr Solzhenitsyn (a captain in the Soviet Red Army during the Second World War, who later won a Pulitzer Prize for Literature) wrote: "dispel any attempt to glorify war … it is a persistent malignancy in human history."

Throughout life runs this dark thread of tragedy and suffering. A power working in nature or in history that can break a person's life, to defeat and destroy. And we all experience this to some degree or another – if not now, then sometime.

Philosopher Kahlil Gibran wrote in his poem on *Joy and Sorrow*: "Together they come and when one sits, alone with you at your board, remember that the other is asleep upon your bed."

How many times have you heard the expression used to describe what is happening to somebody else or what is happening to you: "it's a terrible cross to bear?" For every life, sooner or later, has crosses to bear. We are linked together, bothers and sisters, by the common fact of suffering.

There are, of course, different kinds of crosses. There are those, which strike some as unnecessary. Those, which come to people because of their own limitations in life. Maybe, they manage things poorly and look out on the wreck of their lives to see a tangle of faulty judgments and impulses.

Or, there are inevitable crosses, which come to so many; simply, because we live in an inter-related world. It would take a Tolstoy, I believe, to do justice to the dramas of human lives; which have been affected irrevocably by wider events. Think of hospitals filled with veterans, or innocent New Yorkers, or marathoners, or concertgoers, or school children – who were simply in the wrong place at the wrong time. And whose lives have been hurt or ended by forces beyond their control.

These are the inevitable crosses, which come despite what promise we may have in us. Despite what personal excellence or achievement we may possess. Forces larger than us affect us profoundly: terrorism, wars, recessions, and even unemployment. A virus or a cancer comes along and strikes us unaware. And suddenly, we are laid low; victimized through no fault of our own.

There are crosses, which are simply inevitable – part of the fabric of living. As the remarkable Swiss theologian, Father Hans Küng notes: "There is a kind of cross built into the structure of human life, more difficult than a single heroic act. It is the endurance of ordinary, normal, everyday suffering … the cross of daily life. To take up the cross is to go one's own way in the midst of the risks of one's own situation and uncertain of the future."

In short, we all have crosses to bear. People may resist them nobly, or even foolishly try to deny their reality, but they are there to be borne.

And there is another kind of cross bearing, too. And that is life's voluntary crosses. It's the cross, which comes to a person who simply cannot remain indifferent to someone else's need or suffering.

Scripture is replete with appeals to voluntary cross bearing. Galations 6:5, "Bear ye one another's burdens." Or Romans 15:1, "We then that are strong ought to bear the infirmities of the weak. " Or, Matthew 25:40, "Inasmuch as ye have done unto one of the least of these my brethren, ye do it unto me."

There are men and women, like Mother Teresa of Calcutta, who said, "If you judge people, you have no time to love them."

And others who, through long centuries and even now, have formed a fellowship of caring, of giving, of helping other cross bearing folk. And, paradoxically, their witness is that they have found, in so doing, strength and fulfillment. So, the 12th Century abbot, Bernard of Clairvaux exclaimed: "O blessed burden that makes all burdens light; O blessed yoke that bears the bearer up!"

This is the way of Jesus. Have you ever pondered the strange fact that the same Jesus who said of His mission in John 10:10, "I am come that they might have life, and that they might have it more abundantly," also said in Mark 8:34, "Whosoever will come after me, let him deny himself, and take up his cross, and follow me."

In other words, Jesus is saying that authentic life, life lived at its richest and deepest, is also a life where one bears crosses. This may strike many as absurd. Other great religious teachers have resisted such talk. They would have us avoid pain, minimize risk, find detachment, back away from this dark side of human experience.

But Jesus uses the inevitable cross for love.

It is a creative response. And, in my own life, I've seen this creative response resonating in the lives of so many people. Because of their own suffering, able to reach out to others with understanding and with greater compassion. People who have become less judgmental about the failings of others are more capable of empathetic affirmation. People have taken second or third best and made a life out of it; although along the way, they experienced broken dreams and personal crucifixions.

Have you not known such people, too, and felt the awe of holy wonder?

Yet, it is more than a heroic example, which Jesus gives us. By his own cross bearing, Jesus has released a great power into a world peopled by cross bearers of all kinds.

What is that power? Nothing other than that God, himself, is involved with us in our situation and able to overcome the worst that can be thrown at Him or us. That the One, whom Jesus called Father, is not some remote spectator on the agonies of our lives; that our struggles and our cross bearing is somehow His agony, too. That nothing can separate people from His active love.

If we knew – any of us really knew – the kind of suffering which exists for one moment in this world of crosses, I think our hearts should break. But the cross of Jesus tells us that God does know from within; identifies with all the suffering, sorrow and sin of all the world through all the long ages.

That's the heart of the eternal – for us – and also with us.

For the cross is empty. Out of the worst suffering, out of the apparent meaninglessness of death and defeat, God is able to bring new life.

The risen Christ, through his abiding Spirit …

Can give us a sense of God's own fellowship in our cross bearing;

Can cleanse and heal those who bear the crosses of guilt and self-remorse;

Can strengthen those who falter under the load of inevitable crosses fashioned through no fault of their own;

Can indeed, still prod people to pick up the burden of love for others. To become involved and give of themselves. And find, paradoxically, not that they are diminished, but enhanced. For they have experienced authentic love.

Prayer: May I find the strength in my own life, Oh Lord, to bear my crosses and help others bear theirs, with grace, dignity and your love.

Amen

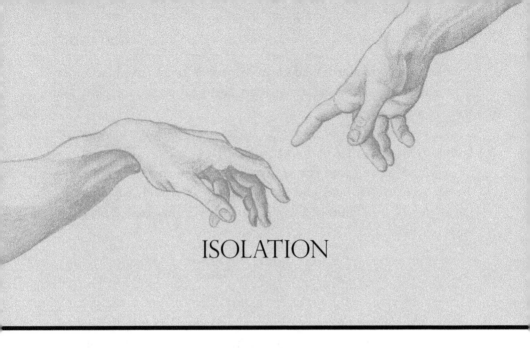

ISOLATION

Our perennial human problem is one of Isolation.

We live in a world of all kinds of barriers – economic, political, and social. Equalitarianism simply does not exist – even in those societies, such as the Soviet Union, which makes such enormous ideological claims. No, there are always barriers.

And the barriers do not easily fall. For example, it took 30 years for the world's most populous nation, China and the world's most advanced industrial nation, the United States to recognize the existence of each other diplomatically.

If it is sometimes slow between nations, how much more at times for individuals. There are periods of estrangement in life, times when people may feel cut off from one another and from God, as did any leper in biblical days.

Leprosy is, indeed, an appropriate metaphor for extreme isolation. It was a horrible condition. And although now curable, ancient society had no remedy for it. Therefore, the leper was kept isolated in order to protect society. There is the heroic story of Father Damien of Molokai in Hawaii who himself died of leprosy at age 49 after caring for the leper colony for 16 years. Until the 1980's, isolation was all that could be done, and that done pretty cruelly.

The Old Testament saw leprosy as disease, and disease as a manifestation of sin. So the leper was considered doubly contagious. Forbidden to have any contact with family or friends, forced to live outside the walls, cut off even from religious activities and from the comfort of sacramental life.

In the opening chapter of Mark's Gospel, Mark 8:1-3, a leper comes one day before Jesus in Galilee and cries out for a miraculous intervention, for healing. "Lord, if thou wilt, thou canst make me clean."

There is hope in that statement. Hope that is grounded in some sort of confidence that this Jesus has the power to heal, to restore, to make clean again -- word had gotten around Galilee about that. But there is also the agony of doubt -- doubt that Jesus will want to bother, to care enough about this isolated, disfigured person from who others shielded their eyes.

That may be, where this story joins our story, too. We may believe, somehow, that God is there – able to straighten out the crooked things, which bother us, to restore us to ourselves.

Yes, but does He really want to? Does He care enough? Particularly, when sometimes we are so low that we wonder what possible use we could be to anyone – let alone an abstraction called God.

Like it or not, that utilitarian standard of self worth is built into us: we are worthwhile, we believe, only if we are useful. There are times in our lives when we do experience a sense of isolation and deep loneliness. We should not be surprised by this; it is not alien, but intrinsic to the human condition.

Paul Tillich, widely regarded as one of the most influential theologians of the 20th Century, said "The character of human life, like the character of the human condition, like the character of all life, is <u>ambiguity</u>. The inseparable mixture of good and evil, the true and false, the creative and destructive forces – both individual and social."

In this ambiguous life, there are times when we find ourselves cut off. Left outside the walls of ordinary human involvement and engagement – emotionally, spiritually, and socially. When invisible barriers accentuate our sense of loneliness.

It may be waking up one fine day in your thirties, forties or fifties and finding that you've indeed made it. You've climbed the ladder of success, you have a position of prestige. And, suddenly, you experience the most profound loneliness! For in climbing there, you put emotional distance between yourself and others. You had to do it, of course. You simply didn't have time for personal involvement if you were going to stay focused and meet your personal goals.

Microsoft founder, Bill Gates readily acknowledges that the person he is today is not one he would have recognized when he was in his 20s and single-mindedly building a company. "I was a zealot," he said. "I didn't believe in weekends. I didn't believe in vacations. I knew everyone's license plate, so I knew when they were coming and going, too. That was my life: doing great software."

Now that you've made it – what have you made?

What resources are there for reconnecting in that moment? If you will, if you want to … you can, cries the leper. If ….

The good news is that Jesus does not merely wish the leper well and then send him on his way with words of cheer. No. Rather, Jesus violates the law and touches the unclean flesh as Matthew continues, "Jesus puts forth his hand and touched him, saying, "I will. Be thou clean. And immediately his leprosy was cleansed."

Jesus runs the risk of contagion by touching one who is outlawed, isolated, dis-eased. He doesn't pray for him. He touches him – and thereby restores the man to health, to the possibility of communion with his family, friends and community.

In a sense, none of us are ever atheists; for each of us has some sort of god. There is something that concerns us ultimately (if only our own self-preservation); something to which we ascribe worth and value.

But in the welter of various images of gods that we fashion and cherish, comes the story of this particular God, whom we glimpse in Jesus Christ. One who acts, who is moved by compassion. One who reaches out and touches, even at great risk and cost to himself.

This One does not wear sterile, latex gloves, does not keep himself antiseptically clean in the far reaches of abstract thought and arid rationality. Rather, he plunges into the ambiguities of human life. And experiences what we all experience at times – loneliness, rejection, even the agony of death.

He gives himself over to the human experience in its totality. And that is precisely why He is able to say: "Be thou clean."

Only One who is involved in the human experience can speak to it, from within it. Only One for whom the human is not alien can restore the human.

Of course, there's more to this story for us to ponder. Jesus does nothing spectacular and dramatic. No. There is simply a human touch, an ordinary thing, and a few words spoken.

But that's the way the One whom we glimpse in Jesus works – in very simple and pedestrian ways. And that suggests why such ordinary sights as a makeshift manger and a simple cross become comforting and abiding metaphors for the highest expression of love.

God employs ordinary things, the ordinary experience of life to make known his extraordinary love. God does his work of reconciliation in such ordinary, unassuming ways. And somehow, we know this in our experience, too.

It is through the intervention of love – the touch, the presence of someone who knows and someone who cares – that we are lifted from our estrangements.

When we experience the depths – the dark sides of our own existence – when we are weighted down with a sense of failure and isolation. What we desperately need, then, is not someone to come along who has all the answers, who can give us new theories, reasons, patterns and prescriptions.

But rather, someone who brings us the touch of caring, quiet presence. A presence, which says "I know it's different, but somehow I've sort of been there, too. And I know how awful it can be." Someone who intervenes positively, simply by being with us. That's the extraordinary power of as ordinary a thing as human touch, a simple sign of care and love.

The deepest truth of which we can speak about God, writes John, the Apostle, is that God is love: that is active, personally involved, seeking, touching. So much so that He comes and enters the human experience and calls forth a community in order to reflect that love. To participate in that love, and to share it through supportive presence with one another and, indeed, with all people.

If that is the deepest truth, then the deepest sin may consist in giving up on other people. To disdain the human condition cynically – as unworthy of the effort – because it is leprous with pain and hurts and marred by ugliness.

The One who comes in Christ loves with a love stronger than all which defaces humanity – and bids us to live in that love.

In a surprising turn, roughly two decades into his tenure at Microsoft, Mr. Gates shifted his attention — and ultimately more than $30 billion of his fortune — to philanthropy. With his wife, Melinda; he has created reportedly the largest private foundation in the nation to improve health in developing countries and to expand opportunities for advancement among those least advantaged in the US.

Prayer: Thank you, Lord, for coming to show me how to touch the people of my life with your love.

Amen

LEAVING HOME

There comes a time for all of us, when we must leave home. Do you remember that time for you?

For some, it may have meant leaving something/somewhere poor and hardscrabble, striking out for that which you had never had – a sense of freedom and dignity.

But for most, I suspect, it was a time of mixed feelings and scrambled emotions. Sadness in moving out from the dear, the familiar, the known and supportive. Yet, excitement, too, that nonetheless we ourselves were doing it; making our own way, coming of age, proving ourselves, becoming our person.

Strange creatures, we. For who can forget the pull of the heart toward home? As Robert Frost penned, "Home is the place where, when you have to go there, they have to take you in."

And yet, who does not know deep within the promptings for something more. Creatures who, in the words of British author, G.K. Chesterton "… are homesick in their homes and strangers under the sun." People who must leave home.

So, it happens for us all. And it happens because nothing is ever static in life. Seasons come and seasons go. And we must come and go, too. And in this process, we must make choices.

I don't mean those more or less relatively trivial choices – such as deciding what kind of car to buy, or where to spend a summer vacation. But basic choices. Those, which shape our lives, which move us this way – and not that; which cause us to be here – and not there.

And the amazing thing, I find, about such basic, fundamental choices is that they are wrapped in a certain shroud of mystery. It's been said that life is a pinball machine. Where you end up, very uncertain.

Why is it that you chose one school and not another? Because, perhaps, a friend happened to nudge you this way or someone happened to intervene for you that way. And you found yourself there in that place – and not some other – and your life was forever different.

Why was it that, new in town, you happened to accept a casual dinner invitation and the only other guest turned out to be this striking person. And while you weren't really ready for some new relationship, something began to happen. And from that point on, your life was changed forever.

The choices we make, the basic choices, of what we will do with our lives or with whom we will share them, are often surrounded by apparently random circumstances. And yet, in retrospect, they may seem not so random at all. But strangely -- if they are the right choices -- fitting and destined.

In the traditional wedding service, there is a prayer, which speaks these words: "As Thou hast brought them together by Thy providence, now sanctify them by Thy Spirit."

Out of all the swarms of people in the world, two have chosen each other. And the prayer – speaking of the providence of God – points toward the deep mystery, which brackets and intertwines our lives, and surrounds our choices. And our response to providential mystery always involves faith, for we step out into the unknown, we risk without certainty.

But when we make this choice. When we leave home and plunge into the unknown; we also walk on a path toward <u>knowing</u>, in a way that is different from reason or calculation. We discover that there are some things in life – and they may be the most important things – which cannot be known by research or reflection. But only by committing ourselves.

We must dare in order to know. We respond in faith to know, to understand. We trust in order to grasp – or be grasped.

You do not come first to understand a person fully and then to love that person. But love somehow comes first – and then it is out of the love that understanding is born.

"Follow me, and I will make you fishers of men," Jesus said to the rough-hewn fishermen, Simon Peter and Andrew and the brothers, James and John as recorded in Matthew 4:19.

The words were spoken then. But they are spoken yet, sounding down the long centuries. And they are linked with our names, too. We, too are beckoned to come, to follow, to know Him by walking with Him. And there are no guarantees – except the pleasure of His company and the companionship of others.

Where will our following take us? Well, **God knows**. And we can be sure only that it will take us probably not where we want to go. But strangely, where we are wanted or needed.

It may take us to a place or a time, when we have to make some difficult choices. Precisely, because we have gained something along the way; a different perspective, a sense of deeper compassion for others. Precisely, because we have not journeyed alone.

But in His company, we have learned some things – fundamental things, basic things about ourselves – and life itself. How life is infinitely precious and must be affirmed in its richness, beyond question or doubt. How life is worth the struggle to defend its dignity. How far God has gone in Christ to reclaim it, at what cost, at what love?

And so, we may come to a time or a place where we are needed – or wanted. And we have to take a stand, make a witness for the very things we have learned along the way. And this may place us at odds with colleagues we admire and with systems we value. That is where following Him may take us one fine day.

And you can be sure that wherever it takes you, it will inevitably cost you something. You'll have to give of yourself, your care, your energy, your time, your money. There is no other way. That's why, at another time, when Jesus beckoned people to leave home in Matthew 16:24 he said: " If any man will come after me … come take up your cross and follow me."

Yet, strangely, when we do respond – when we do give, we find at some level our own fulfillment, too. We are enhanced, not diminished. In giving ourselves for Christ, we also receive ourselves in a new way. Which points to something else which we carry with us. Or take with us inevitably – when we leave home on a journey to where we do not know.

And that is knowledge of our own unendingly ambiguous motives. A recognition that even in our best, most generous actions – even done in His name and for His sake – there remains always something in it for us! It is said that we all listen to WII-FM, What's In It For Me? That none of us seems to have the purity of heart, the pure love of God, for others.

No. Yet, the good news is that we <u>can</u> follow – that we <u>can</u> act, despite the inexorable self-centeredness, which is intertwined in all of our activities. For the voice does not say to us: First be sure that your motives are pure and selfless – and then follow me.

The voice we hear is the One which summoned Peter and Andrew, James and John -- who used to quarrel boisterously as to which one should be first in the kingdom; which one should sit at the head of the table at the messianic feast.

Which means what? That we do not have to belong – anyone of us – to a spiritual elite in order to be counted as the sons and daughters of God. We do not have to master some new esoteric vocabulary to be counted as those worthy of His love and grace. We do not have to enslave ourselves to a new set of rigid rules and regulations.

We can accept our human condition realistically – its grandeur and misery -- its capacity for greatness and pettiness – for generosity and gain. We can accept the truth about ourselves – and still journey along.

And that leads to this question: how shall we go? It would be wonderful to say that we go joyously, happily, following the Master. But that is not always the case. For sometimes, we drag ourselves along, wishing that we had never heard the summons. Sometimes, we think that we would rather be done with the whole affair.

But the voice persists. And we hear it again with clarity, when we encounter someone who needs us. Or a situation that shocks us into realizing that there are forces, which stand opposed to everything that Christ means for the human race.

And it is then, again, that we turn once more to the strength which others in His company offer us: to the church. The "people of the way" is the curious title by which Christians first designated themselves – people who are following, walking along with Him.

That's you and me and all others who take His name. We are His church. Which also means that we are His body – a weak thing in most ways, half-hearted and of little faith at times, but full of hope for all that.

And the only body that He now has in this world, the only hands and feet to do His work. And such is His power that even through us, others may be led to follow, too.

Prayer: Let me follow where you lead, oh Lord!

Amen

LOST & FOUND

How many ways are there to be lost in this world? More, I think, than you or I could ever imagine. People get lost in spirals of violence. People get lost through nature's tumultuous disasters. People get lost because of their folly.

An erstwhile pop queen marks her tentative return to a public performance fiasco, in which she teeters though her dance steps. And mouths only occasional words in a sad attempt to lip-sync her new single, "Gimme More." She is a lost soul – lost in the sad culture of celebrity.

Conversely, people get lost in brave acts of serving others. Remember the terrible day of September 11, 2001? We remember not only the victims, but also the heroes who were lost trying to help others. The first victim was a beloved Catholic priest in New York, Father Mychal Judge, who's ministry was in a far-flung flock, including the homeless, AIDS patients and alcoholics, firefighters and paralyzed police officers.

He, too, was lost serving the Lord and his parishioners.

People can get lost literally even when they appear to have everything going for them. An article in London's Sunday Telegraph tells about successful young men described as "The Metropolitan Smart Set: thirty-something, fat salaries, expensive clothes and glossy lives. But beneath it all lie some tortured souls." And the article bears the title, *The Lost Boys*.

Lost boys – lost celebrities – lost martyrs.

People do get lost in life; lost sometimes because they are simply in harm's way, in the march of human evil, or the catastrophes of nature.

Have you ever been lost, really lost?

It can happen you know, strangely, even in a crowd.

Sometimes you can get lost, even in the midst of your own family.

You can be lost when someone may ask about you, and you dodge, saying nothing of your own sense of lostness; for fear that you might only exacerbate your sense of shame and alienation.

Jesus came seeking the lost.

Writes Luke in his Gospel 15:1-2, "they drew near unto Him all the publicans (tax collectors) and sinners for to hear Him. And the Pharisees and the scribes murmured saying, 'This man receiveth sinners and eateth with them.'"

The tax collectors were fellow Jews who, on behalf of Rome, collected taxes from their oppressed brothers and sisters. It was all done on a commission basis, in which they received a portion of the taxes that they collected – a system inviting corruption and injustice.

The "sinners" were people who were careless of all the scruples of the religious and ceremonial law, which carried both ritualistic and moral constraints and obligations.

Now, Jesus was a realist. These people – tax collectors and sinners – were indeed "lost!" That is, they were cut off from society. They were judged and found wanting. They were outsiders, estranged from their own. They had violated their own traditions; they had dishonored their own heritage. They were unacceptable and lost.

Some were surely lost by their folly – just as a sheep is lost – not so much, perhaps by deliberate, willful acts, but through distraction.

A rancher once explained how sheep stray, "They just nibble themselves lost. They keep their heads down, wander from one green tuft to another, come to a hole in the fence, and never can find the hole by which to get back again."

And are we not all like sheep gone astray at times, getting lost through carelessness; through forgetting boundaries, following the allure of grass which is always greener on the other side?

Think of how easy it is to succumb at times to peer pressure, to give way to the herd mentality and instinct. Have you ever succumbed? Who hasn't, if in subtle ways, so strong is the push for conformity.

And it begins early, this desire not to be different. The fear to stand out, not fit in. So go along, try not to be noticed. That's middle school, that's high school.

There are many ways to get lost. It's not just careless sinners or acquisitive tax collectors.

It's also the people who condemn them so bitterly, the Pharisees, the scribes and the elder righteous stay-at-home brothers who refuse to welcome and embrace the lost. How do these straight shooters get lost? Well, by their pretensions; that they are somehow morally exempt from the human condition of finitude, folly, rebellion and sin.

They get lost because of the pretension that their righteousness provides a kind of moral immunity to the tragic reality of our sad humanity. We can get lost very easily along the paths of self-righteousness, can't we? And condemnation of others in the name of some abstraction, some unremitting demand for purity? But this recognition must lead to humility – to an awareness that ultimately we live by grace alone.

We are all the more estranged and lost if we cannot recognize our own capacity for estrangement, our own incompleteness, and our own precarious stance in the slippery business of living. Don't we sometimes identify with the haunting lyrics of the song, *They Call the Wind Maria*: "And now I'm lost, so … lost. Not even God can find me."

Jesus came, He once said, to seek and to save the lost. That is, to reclaim people for their true destiny as children of the loving Father. To reconnect them to the Father. So, He befriends sinners. He eats with them, despite the moral outrage of others.

And He does so for two reasons. First, He regards them as centers of value, bearers of God's own image. That is, able to relate to God and to others in love. And secondly, He looks upon their lostness with God's own compassion.

What does that mean for you and me? Just this: that even though you and I may have gotten lost along the paths of our lives, even though you and I <u>do</u> get lost. Nonetheless, we are sought as we are, where we are. The God, who refuses to give up, seeks you and me, again and again. God is not done with us.

Each of us is sought. Sometimes we become aware of our need, strangely, only in the dislocation of our lives. When something happens to us that plunges us suddenly into a lonely place; where we are aware of our aloneness and vulnerability and need. Then, we are aware of our inability, our infirmities of the soul, where we are lost.

And we discover by grace that we are not alone. There is One who, by the Spirit, searches for us, finds us and says, Come walk with me. I am here to guide you through the waters of grief.

He seeks us in our lostness; in those very places where, in our brilliance, we may have hidden ourselves too well. Which points to the mystery of being found. A coin scarcely finds itself. Sheep never can discern the path back.

But there is great rejoicing when the search for them is fruitful. Again and again in our lives, the drama is acted out. We are found anew with a deeper sense of the mystery of it all.

There is a joy, which comes when lost folk are found. When people are reconnected again with a self that they've lost somewhere along the way. When they experience the presence of the Seeker in this mist of their estrangement and can find a future again. A future marked by compassion. So that now, they are more open to care for others, who may be lost, too. More open to those who bear the lonely pains of being human in all its extremes.

In Christ, God comes to where you live and move and have your being. Even into the depths, the lonely places of your life, even into the darkness of your shame and self-loathing. He seeks to bring new life; through embracing you, wounds and all. One who seeks to bring love. That you may know the joy that causes us to sing, *Amazing Grace*:

Amazing Grace, How sweet the sound
That saved a wretch like me
I once was lost, but now am found
T'was blind, but now I see

Prayer: Oh Lord, find me in the midst of my sadness and aloneness.
Amen

101

LOVING & HURTING

One summer, the Los Angeles Times ran an article by the Pulitzer Prize-winning, syndicated columnist George F. Will entitled, *"Rain, why are you always fallin' strictly on my little ol' parade?"*

It was an apt title, for it caught the flavor of Will's column. It seems that on a recent trip to Denver, he had decided to indulge in a bit of pop anthropology. And so had repaired to several saloons that featured "country" music. More than the music or beat, he paid particular attention to the lyrics.

And if the words of the various ballads reflected anything of what life was really like for "country" folk, then he could only conclude that life was pretty dismal. He pieced together – from various songs – this picture of the misfortune, which attends typical "country" lives:

"You wore my high school ring and letter sweater before bright, bright neon lights made you up and walk away from standing by your man.

"Leaving the crops in the field and me jamming gears with nothing to do but keep on trucking in my 18-wheeler.

"Listening to the windshield wipers when I'm not drinking Falstaff and Wild Turkey and putting the last dime from my faded jeans into a jukebox to help me make it through the night.

"Wishing I could make the alimony payments and visit little Billie and Betsy Sue.

"So in Elko, Nevada Greyhound depot I shot the man, my best friend, who took you and even my pickup truck.

"And I wound up here on Death Row, listening to the lonesome whistle of the night train rolling south through the cotton fields from Nashville to that little bit of heaven, Biloxi."

And so on.

Then Will comments: "Well, now, if such lyrics are an accurate survey of the bucolic life then life hurts like the dickens. We might as well admit that civilization has come a cropper (ruin) and the fabric of society is unraveling, even in the country. But there is this to be said for the forthright sorrowfulness of country music. It is a timely assertion of an endangered right -- the right to be unhappy."

Leo Rosten, an American humorist and Yiddish lexicographer also champions the "ability to be unhappy" soundly, without apology or rationalization. "Once upon a time -- very long ago -- a man could stare glumly out of a window, or grunt at his wife, or slam the door, or stalk off on a solitary walk. Without having his loved ones rush to his rescue with bright psychiatric phrases and psycho-therapy handy-dandy. Once upon a time -- believe it or not -- we were not silly enough to expect everyone to walk around in a state of bliss. Or give hourly demonstrations of being well-adjusted. Once upon a time -- oh, blessed time! -- sensible folk simply knew that life, even at its best, is beset with difficulties. That frustration or disappointment or defeat is natural and as inevitable as changes in the weather. That men (and presumably women) were permitted the dignity of periodic discontent."

Rosten went on to say: "The purpose of life is not to be happy—but to matter, to be productive, to be useful, to have it make some difference that you lived at all."

Obviously, these words appealed to me. For I found it kind of corrective to that romantic notion to which a good many of us try to cling. That someday, bye and bye -- maybe next week or the week after that --surely life is going to become reasonably smooth and harmonious. So that we will neither inadvertently hurt those about whom we care or be profoundly hurt by them.

But the truth of course, even if it is dramatically overstated in country music, is that everything hurts somebody sometimes. Try as we may, there seems to be no way out of this common human predicament.

Some people, of course, do try. They try to insulate themselves from any chance of possibly being hurt by distancing themselves emotionally from other people. Having been hurt, they are afraid of being hurt again. And so, avoid the risk of entering any relationship deeply; not allowing themselves to become vulnerable to the emotional pain, which someone close to them might afflict.

A few years ago, one of the world's wealthiest men, commenting on his numerous marriages, said in an interview: "I've always tried to avoid being hurt. It doesn't do you any good, letting a woman get to you that badly. And I've been pretty much successful, I think."

Perhaps so. But he's paid a price – more precious than his money – for trying to become invulnerable to emotion's pain. For to be involved in any significant way with someone else; always means that we invest ourselves, our energies, our affections, our passions and time. And in doing so, become vulnerable.

We become vulnerable to misunderstandings and to cuts. And it hurts. It hurts deeply. And we feel very alone and wonder how it is that we can suddenly be such strangers.

It happens all the time – between spouses, between friends, between lovers. For love and trust – when they are real – make us lower our guard and open our real self to another. And we become most defenseless with those whom we love most, those whom we need most, and with whom we share the most.

That is why the pain we feel is then the most intense. Because we really don't have our defenses up and there is nothing to shield us from the blow of misunderstanding. Or what seems to us as callous indifference to our needs.

And we can't just laugh it off, or ignore it, or distract ourselves from this kind of pain. Sometimes there is nothing, apparently, we can do except feel it, experience it.

And there are no glib answers to this predicament, no easy salves to soothe away the pain of being human. Nonetheless, there are some resources, which, as Christians, we can appropriate and utilize.

One is the perception – at such times when we ourselves are

hurting – that this is surely the way the persons whom we love feel, when, for one reason or another, we have hurt them. We need to remember that although we really hadn't intended to harm them – nonetheless, we had. So, we know what it feels like – from the inside.

Another is that we are not perfect. We are finite people in a finite world, and we are all tainted with our own narrow perspectives. And our own inevitable self concern, even with people who are near and dear to us.

And so, we go right on doing it all the time – delivering those cuts that we really wouldn't consciously want -- at our finer, more aware moments -- to own or claim.

And that perception – knowing what it feels like from the inside – may serve as a prod to a heightened awareness of just how lethal our own thoughtlessness can be. And, therefore, it may help us deal more compassionately with the one who has wounded us.

Another resource is this: the healing power, which Jesus kept insisting is in wholehearted forgiveness. As He said from his own cross of pain and humiliation (Luke 23:34) "Father, forgive them. For they know not what they do."

As American psychologist, Eugene Kennedy wrote: "Forgiveness demands that we make ourselves open to getting hurt all over again. That asks a great deal from each of us. Much more than a quick 'mea culpa' or an embarrassed wish that we would forget that this or that has happened. Forgiveness comes from people who have hurt each other, but are willing, out of the love that gives them that awful power still, to run the risk that it may happen again. That is, the only remedy there is for the hurts that we give to one another."

Thus, the paradox of love. When we love, we open ourselves in trust and longing; we become accessible to one another. And are therefore, vulnerable, targets for each other's insensitivity and misunderstanding.

Yet, it is the power of love, which allows us to be open to the renewing power of forgiveness. And which strengthens us and helps us hold on in a life where everyone gets hurt sometimes. There is a grace, which operates in our loving and being hurt and hurting that makes reconciliation possible.

The force of this power struck me anew when I read an episode in the Los Angeles Times by the beloved columnist, Jack Smith. He and his wife had taken a trip to Northern California, and in Sacramento searched out the old Victorian house where they had lived as newlyweds.

As they sat in the car, thinking back over the years, he said: "That's it. There's the bedroom window back there, where I stood outside in the rain that night you wouldn't let me in."

"I don't remember that," she said.

"How strange that was," I thought. "Though people have lived together most of their lives, one of them may vividly remember a shared experience that the other has quite forgotten. Evidently, my being shut out in the rain that night had not been as important to her as it had to me. I had felt guilty about that night for 35 years, and for no reason: she didn't even remember it."

We hurt and are hurt. But that is the price of being related, the price of loving and caring; of investing ourselves and becoming vulnerable. But there is the power of tenacious love, which Jesus taught and demonstrated, which brings forgiveness and helps us to begin again.

Prayer: "Dear Lord, let me stop hurting and heal my pain with the gift of forgiveness."

Amen

OUR NEED TO REMEMBER

In T.S. Elliott's play, *The Cocktail Party,* an unidentified and strangely wise guest offers this advice to an estranged couple:

> "Don't," he says, "strangle each other with knotted memories."

How often we have seen relationships eroded and eventually destroyed by an obsession with bitter episodes from the past; with the rehearsal and replaying of mutual hurts, disappointments and conflicts. We need to learn to know what and how to forget – if we are to press on toward a meaningful future.

Yet, to know what and how to forget is only a half-truth. The other half lies in knowing what to remember.

In an ancient Greek legend, a woman comes down to the River Styx to be ferried across to the region of departed spirits.

Charon, the kindly ferryman, reminds her that she may now drink of the waters of Lethe and thus forget the life she is leaving.

Eagerly, she asks, "I will forget how I have suffered?"

And, replies Charon, "Remember, too, that you will forget how you have rejoiced."

The woman exalts, "I will forget my failures?"

The old ferryman adds, "And your victories."

She continues: "I will forget how I have been hated?"

"And also, how you have been loved," Charon responds.

There are, you see, some things in your past; which ought never be forgotten. In John 14:26, Jesus promised the Holy Spirit, God's continuing presence to His disciples for years to come:

"He shall teach you all things, and bring all things to your remembrance."

Memories, then, are important ... and need to be cherished.

One of the most beloved preachers of the 20th Century, John H. Jowett once said: "I suppose that one of the most urgent needs of the common life is the sanctification of memory. If memory were to be really hallowed, it would forget many things which it now remembers; and it would certainly remember many things it now forgets."

What, then, should we remember?

We ought to remember – all of us – those special experiences, which strengthened us or in which we strengthened others.

All of us have lived lives rich in human experience. We have all known the heights and depths of human existence. We all have significant and important stories to tell. One of the tragedies of our youth-oriented society is the fact that so many people dismiss or ignore the older person; who often, has deeply moving and illuminating experiences to share.

In the lives of all of us, there are times which deserve to be treasured; to be recalled into the present, relived, gathered-again, remembered.

Times when we accomplished something against great odds; times when we conquered over a persistent deficiency; times when we were touched by a sense of awe at the mystery and majesty of life itself. When we heard great music, or saw a great beauty or knew a great love.

In the Book of Exodus 16:33, we are told that Moses commanded Aaron to take a jar and put a measure of manna in it for generations to come, a sacred token of the remembrance of God's great goodness.

So, we need these tokens of memory.

A great professor, fumbling in his pocket for a coin, brought out a pebble. Looking at it, he said: "My little boy picked that up and gave it to me on our last walk before I left home, and I have carried it around the world."

A pebble becomes a passport to a remembered life. So, we need to keep our scrapbooks, our photographs, the delightful drawings made by young hands. Why?

Because in our past are many fine and precious hours. And to forget them means to impoverish all of our tomorrows. To remember the best of the past is to find strength for the future.

Do you remember Britain's magnificent stand against the Nazi tyranny in the summer of 1941; when she stood alone against the pagan hordes of Hitler? Where did she summon courage? Logic would have dictated a defeatist attitude. But here was defiance and determination. Where did it come from?

The prominent American journalist, Edward R. Murrow, covering the scene from London, said: "Unconsciously, they dug deep into their history and felt that Drake, Raleigh, Hawkins, Cromwell and all the rest were looking down at them. And they were obliged to look worthy in the eyes of their ancestors."

Churchill was to say, "This was England's finest hour." And it was memory that provided the deep wellspring for courage.

On the night, when he was facing betrayal -- with death only a few hours away -- Jesus took bread, blessed it and broke it, saying to His disciples in 1 Corinthians 11:24: Take, eat: this is my body, which is broken for you. Do this in remembrance of me."

So ever since, Christians have gathered at the Lord's Supper – and in taking bread – remembered that there once lived a man, both righteous and loving. Both bound to serve and yet free, who showed us what it means to be human and what God's love is all about. And in that remembrance, we find strength to live life now – to let His life enter our lives. Become renewed for the great task of reconciliation in the world.

The brilliant film, *The Parable* was first screened at the World's Fair in 1964. And since, has been selected by the Library of Congress for preservation in the U.S. National Film Registry for its cultural, historical or aesthetic significance. In it, the world is portrayed as a parade – a circus, in all of its movement, color, excitement and gaudiness.

Christ is shown as a clown – absurd perhaps because he does that which the world counts as real folly – he lives for others. He quietly liberates people who have come to think that there is no other way for them to live.

Near the end of the film, after the clown has been strung up and put to death – the people who have been helped by Him gather silently on a grassy knoll.

It is all over.

But, as they begin to remember, as they recall the impact of his life upon their lives – they see something startling.

Through the distant trees, there comes a flash of color and motion. The circus is moving out, on down the road. The wagons, decorated in the symbols of all the nations of the world, bump along.

They watch as the train turns the bend and disappears out of sight.

But, as they remember the One who touched their lives with healing and hope, they see the clown again; following on a donkey, not giving up, still traveling, still going after the world, quietly and without fanfare making his way.

In their remembering, they see clearly the greatest truth of life; a love that will not give up, a love that will persist, a love that lives.

The old psalmist in Psalms 103:1-2 said it: "Bless the Lord. O my soul, and all that is within me. Bless His holy name! Bless the Lord, O my soul, and forget not all His benefits."

There are some things in life we must never forget. Cherish your memories that strengthen.

Prayer: Dear Lord, let me remember from my yesterdays all that will enrich my tomorrows.

Amen

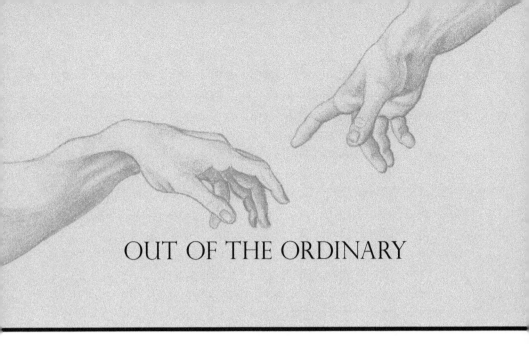

OUT OF THE ORDINARY

As every Sunday school child learns, there are four gospels in the Bible ---
Matthew, Mark, Luke and John --- which tell the story of Jesus' life and
ministry. But every Bible student soon learns, there are great differences
between these witnesses. And especially so, between John's Gospel and
the others.

The very moment you read the first words of John's gospel, you know
that you are entering into a more poetic, philosophic, symbolic landscape.
Echoing the opening words of the Bible, "In the beginning," he writes in
John 1:1, "In the beginning was the Word and the Word was with God,
and the Word was God. …" It is a hymn, a poem speaking of God's
universal longing to speak with those who are made in His image.

But when this great prologue ends, what follows? Well, no metaphysical
theme. Rather, a simple – indeed, almost trivial – kind of story, in which
there is a wedding at a village called Cana in Galilee. And, embarrassingly,
the wine runs out.

In Palestine, at that time, a village wedding was a real occasion.
Weddings lasted seven days. The people of the community participated as
they found the time, and so new guests arrived each day.

First was the wedding ceremony, followed by a meal, after which the
couple would proceed to their new home in a torch light procession. Guests
and friends would lead them on the longest, most winding route – so that

everyone in the village might be able to share in the well-wishing of this new family. It would be similar to the horn-honking parade of cars, which often follows a wedding in our own day.

That whole week, when guests gathered to celebrate, the couple would open their home to them. They, in turn, would be treated royally all that time.

Into this kind of happy occasion came Jesus and his newest disciples, Philip and Nathanael. The feast was already in its third day – and, as the story suggests, the supply of wine was running low. Wine was, of course, an essential to such festivities. To run out of wine was to ruin the party and to suffer great embarrassment.

When Jesus' mother, Mary, discovered the shortage, she appealed to Jesus and instructed the servants to do as He said. Jesus calls for empty stone pots and adds the most common substance, water.

And the maitre d' of the day was surprised by the fine quality of the wine now presented to him. For normally, such a fine wine would have been offered first – while the guests' tongues were most sensitive. Later, when people were into the party, a less expensive wine could be served.

Nothing could be more realistic than this touch in the story. It's exactly what happens at many parties today. If there's going to be a lot of wine drunk, serve the good stuff first! Later on, no one will notice you are serving "vin ordinaire." On that almost humorous note, the story ends.

Jesus performed this first of his mighty works in Cana of Galilee, where He revealed his glory, and His disciples believed in Him.

Well it was, after all, a miracle. Wasn't it? And there is no attempt to explain it. Indeed, the miracle itself isn't really described. It's almost incidental. Merely, that the maitre d' "tasted the water which had turned into wine." That's all.

"The conscious water saw its God and blushed," wrote British poet, Richard Crashaw. But it is obviously not the physical fact we are to focus on, but its meaning.

A miracle is said to be "a wonder with a meaning in it." And certainly, the Cana wonder has meaning in it. And that is, that the wonder-making Lord begins where you are. If you are looking for God, you can do no better than to begin with common things.

What does it value any of us to attempt to explain the world around us and above us, until we have faced the world within us – the world of our own human existence? On this lonely and common ground, we are all equals. Even the most discerning, even the most disciplined of minds, must face what we all face: personal experience.

All equals. With experiences marred by ambiguities. With decisions to be made. With consequences, often beyond our imagining, out of our control.

Living is a risky, personal business. And the first and fundamental wonder, John writes, is that God begins here, too, and uses what he finds.

Jesus begins with empty stone pots and adds the most common substance, water. He identifies with people in their need – threatened with the hurt of embarrassment. And this is a note that runs throughout all four gospels: whenever people are hurting, Jesus responds.

When they are sunk in sin and self-loathing, He forgives them and restores their self-respect. When they are timid, He empowers them. When they are humiliated, He stands beside them. When they are attacked, He defends them. When they are wrong, He rebukes them. But whenever they are hurt, He helps them.

That's one level – an enduring level – to this story.

Now, let's look at this story from another level. For John's Gospel has a curious illumination. The quality -- almost of a dream -- where every gesture, every detail suggests the presence of meaning beneath meaning. People move with a kind of ritual stateliness. Where faces melt into other faces, where voices speak words of elusive, but inexhaustible significance.

We already hear the whisper of that awe-inspiring statement: This is my blood.

In the Bible, blood is life. And here the wine, symbol of new life in Christ, is also the reflection of the life that is being poured out. As He goes on his healing, loving, suffering way to the final sacrifice on the cross.

The author David Read: "The simple story now confronts us with a Christ who loves us unto death. Who transforms the water of a dull and legalistic religion or a shabby secularism into the costly wine of His grace. A Savior, 'whose blood was shed for us.'"

So, what is the take away from this story in John? Well, most powerfully perhaps, the feeling simply of the joy of it all. A wedding which almost flopped except that this strange, tough and tender guest came and turned it into the best of all parties.

And maybe that's the point of it all: that the wonder-making Lord enriches what you have.

Out of ordinary water comes wine – your life enriched.

Out of spiritually flat and stale jars, comes something which sparkles and transforms your life. And it keeps happening, you know, as people encounter the mystery of grace in Jesus Christ. A miracle of change and transformation.

Sometimes, we go for years carrying with us hurts and doubts; hurts and doubts that we carefully try to conceal, so no one will know. Afraid that if any one did, we would suffer even more rejection.

Sometimes, that which liberates, that which changes all of this are ordinary things. Just as ordinary as water. Or words.

John says in 1:14, "The word becomes flesh." In Jesus.

Christ's words bring forgiveness, which allows us to forgive even ourselves. All that burdens us – the fearful and fretful -- that we carry with us for years begins to dissolve. And a new reality of acceptance and self worth begins to emerge. Thankfully, we will never be the same. And neither will those around us, as we become freer, more responsive, less self-imprisoned persons.

We are simple clay pots with lives of water changed into wine. The miracle still goes on. And that has promise for you and me.

Prayer: Dear Lord, let the ordinary in my life become extraordinary as I witness the miracles of your grace.

Amen

RECOVERING SELF-WORTH

"Once upon a time," theologian Donald E. Messer's parable began, as all good stories do. A farmer, while walking through the forest, discovered a young eagle that had fallen from its nest. He took it home with him to nurture and raise it.

The most natural place for him to put it was in the barnyard, where the young eagle was surrounded by chickens. It quickly adapted to its new environment. It ate what the chickens ate and began to behave as the chickens did.

One day, a visiting naturalist came by. He inquired of the farmer why an eagle, king of all birds, should be confined to a barnyard, surrounded by such domesticated, captive creatures as chickens.

The farmer replied that since it had grown up with the chickens, it had never learned to fly. It simply behaves as chickens do, the farmer opined, so it really is no longer an eagle.

The naturalist protested that surely it still had the heart of an eagle and therefore could be taught to fly. Thus, began an intriguing experiment to discover whether it was possible for the eagle to recover its intrinsic nature. Gently, the naturalist took the young bird in his arms and said: "You belong to the sky and not to the earth. Stretch forth your wings and fly."

But the eagle seemed confused. He did not know who he was. And seeing the chickens eating their food, he jumped down to be with them again.

Then, the naturalist took the eagle to the roof of the house. Again, he urged him, saying: "You are an eagle. Stretch forth your wings and fly." But the beautiful creature, afraid of his unknown self and the wider vision of the world around him, jumped down once more for the familiar confines of the barnyard.

Finally, the naturalist rose early and took the eagle out from the farm to a high hill. There, he held the king of birds above him and encouraged him again, saying, "You are an eagle. You belong to the sky as well as to the earth. Stretch forth your wings now and fly."

The eagle looked back toward the barnyard and up to the sky. Still he did not fly. Then the naturalist lifted him straight toward the sun. The eagle began to tremble and slowly stretched his wings. At last, with a triumphant and mighty screech of an eagle, he soared into the heavens.

Dr. Messer commented, "It may be that the eagle still remembers the chickens with nostalgia. It may even be that he occasionally revisits the barnyard. But as far as anyone knows, he never returned to lead the life of a chicken."

Our society is filled with hurting people who have lost touch with their strengths and inner capacities. Ones who see themselves as less than they really are. As less, the Christian message insists, than God sees them.

An eagle, born to be an eagle, king of birds, lived instead as a chicken. So do many of us. We don't see our intrinsic, essential nature as those who are worthwhile, who are valued by the greatest reality, God himself. We settle for an existence, in which we accommodate to a lesser view of ourselves.

How many of us see ourselves, for example, as perpetual losers; victims, rather than as ones who can cope and can summon enormous, indeed soaring strength? And who have a resource beyond ourselves, which helps us liberate the very best we have in us? How many of us are prone to rehearse to ourselves – almost habitually – our sense of failure, of inadequacy?

How many of us speak to ourselves in our secret, inner dialogue in "put-down" terms, punishing ourselves more harshly than we would ever consider judging others?

Now, modern society is replete with all kinds of strategies, techniques, cults – some helpful, some counter-productive – by which people try to find again or to discover for the first time, a sense of well-being and self-worth.

It is the old gospel message – offered freely to everyone who has ears to hear -- which I believe, has the power to help us find ourselves anew as ones who are valued and therefore valuable.

At the heart of that message is the good news that we are loved – loved by One who is tenacious. One whose will for us is indomitable. One who seeks us and values us without counting the cost. "This is love," wrote St. John in Book 1, 4:10, "not that we loved God, but that He loved us …."

Christian faith is not escapism. It helps us face ourselves as we really are. It does not pretend that we do not have our dark sides. That we are, indeed, alienated from ourselves at some deep levels. But it knows something else, as well. That beyond and above everything else that can be said about any one of us, we are valued above everything else in all creation.

As Muriel James, a Christian therapist, wrote, "The fundamental premise is that beneath all the human self-centered pride and sinfulness, beneath all the psychological garbage accumulated in layers of hate, jealousy, anger, anxiety, resentment, envy, lust and the rest; there -- at the bottom of the well -- lies a core of goodness."

We are made in the image of God himself. And because God loves us, seeks us, accepts us as we are; we are free to begin to love ourselves, to affirm ourselves as worthwhile. To accept our limitations, yes – but also to appreciate our strengths. To live with a new sense of freedom and appreciation for the unique people we really are!

Eugene C. Kennedy, a former priest and professor of psychology at Loyola University/Chicago wrote a very helpful little book entitled: *If You Really Knew Me, Would You Still Like Me?* Well, the God who reveals himself in Jesus Christ answers that question unequivocally. Yes! I love you even as you are – less than perfect, with all your knots and quirks and twisted ways.

To those who take Him at his word -- who respond to that Yes! -- who begin to understand that we are loved as we are; He gives the power to grow. To rise above the self-destructive patterns, by which we rehearse the worst – rather than the best – in us.

Flip through the pages of the gospel record and you will be surprised to discover how little time Jesus spent allowing people to expand on their burdened pasts, to rehearse their failures and their feelings of self-worth or lack thereof.

To the adulterous woman thrown at His feet by a judgmental mob,

Jesus didn't demand that she amplify the circumstances that had pushed her to her fall. Rather, He simply took her by the hand and said in John 8:11, "Neither do I condemn thee, go and sin no more."

The Christian message says simply: that it is never too late for a person to begin to discover and affirm his or her worth as a child of God, as a valuable and competent person. It is never too late to begin to grow into a more authentic and joyful life. A life where we can begin to accept ourselves as we are, because we are accepted and loved by One who values us.

DePaul University professor William Muehl once visited a fine ancestral home in Virginia. He followed the aged owner, the last of a distinguished colonial family, as she proudly showed him through her home. An ancient rifle above the fireplace intrigued him. So, he asked if he might take it down and examine it. She replied, "Oh, I'm very sorry. I just can't allow it. You see, it just wouldn't be safe. The rifle is loaded and primed, ready to fire.

"My great-grandfather kept it there in constant readiness against the moment he might strike a blow for the freedom of the colonies." Professor Muehl said: "Oh, then he died before the American Revolution?" "No," came the reply. "He lived to a ripe old age and died in 1802. But he never had any confidence in the general and Commander in Chief, whom he knew as a boy, George Washington."

How many of us, like the ancestor with the loaded gun, hold back and let the great opportunities for an expanded and adventurous life trickle by ... while we keep rehearsing the worst about others and ourselves?

Hear the good news – the liberating news! You are loved. You are accepted. You are free to become the person you are really meant to be. There is One, who both points the way and helps us along. He is the One, who in Jesus Christ summons you and me to the feast, the banquet of life!

Prayer: Dear Lord, let me love and value myself as you love and value, me.

Amen

SAVVY SAINTS

Savvy. Perceptive. Shrewd as in the oft-heard phrase "savvy Washington insiders." But sometimes one can be too shrewd for one's own good, certainly not the good of others.

Some time ago, the Los Angeles Times carried a front-page story with the headline, "Lawsuit King Wins One on His Way to Prison."

And the story began:

"As he negotiated the deal that would send him to prison and seal his disgrace, the King of Class Actions was still working the system."

William L. Lerach agreed to plead guilty to one count of conspiracy, in connection with a kickback scheme that paid people to serve as plaintiffs in lawsuits. But he insisted that the firm he founded in San Diego be shielded from prosecution.

If its reputation as a litigator of class-action suits against which Lerach once called the 'dishonorable and despicable greed' of corporate America could be preserved, maybe a little of his own reputation would be, too.

"'He was 'falling on his sword,' said David Lisi, a corporate defense attorney in Silicon Valley. 'You have to admire loyalty like that.'"

Lerach had been more loathed than admired by corporate executives. He was so effective at shaking awards and settlements loose from companies that he became a verb – as in "getting Ler-ached" – taken by a shrewd operator, a legal insider.

In the Gospel of Luke, Jesus tells his disciples the parable of a dishonest steward who also uses his savvy to save his skin. For he, too, is a cool character; a charming street-wise estate manager. But he is too clever by half, and one fine day he gets caught in the practice of inflating his boss' accounts and pocketing the margin for himself.

Word of his practice gets back to the wealthy landowner and the jig is up. The manager gets called on the carpet and is summarily fired.

"What shall I do?" the steward asks himself in Luke 16:3, "for my lord taketh away from me the stewardship: I cannot dig; to beg I am ashamed."

But the manager pulls victory out of the jaws of defeat. One by one, he summons the tenants (who apparently do not know that he has been fired) and immediately re-negotiates the percent they owe.

As they pay up, it becomes a win/win situation. Everyone is happy. The farmers are delighted to be paying less; the wealthy landowner gets what is actually due him, and the master commends the dishonest manager for his shrewdness. He retains the manager and praises his street smarts, his chutzpah. It all presumably served him well.

Instead of being seen as a common crook, he is now perceived as a Paul Newman kind of character, ever cool, shrewd, a real player.

Now, what are we to make of this?

Sooner or later, we build a life; and we have to affirm a center around which we find meaning. We have to ask who or what is our god, and in whom or what do we place our ultimate trust?

The point of the parable is driven home by Jesus reminding the disciples once again in Luke 16:13: "No servant can serve two masters: for either he will hate the one, and love the other; or else he will hold to the one, and despise the other. Ye cannot serve God and mammon."

Now, mammon is a great biblical word. In a narrow sense, it means money, but it also means something more. It means everything, which the mystique of money conveys: sleekness, autonomy, whatever shapes your dreams.

It is not that mammon is intrinsically bad. It is not. Jesus never condemned wealth in and of itself. What He said is that wealth or any form of mammon doesn't work; if we look to it as a means for our health, our salvation, our wholeness. It just doesn't work. There are limits to what we may possess.

Arnold Bennett, a noted novelist, was rich and renowned. But on his deathbed, in his sumptuous London apartment; he whispered to his mistress, as she bent over his dying form, "It's all gone wrong, my dear."

Somehow, in a world, where we cultivate a center rooted in our own finite power, it all goes wrong. That center cannot hold. Mammon doesn't work. You cannot create a relationship or a society on narrow self-interest alone. Priorities must be established in life. In theological terms, a god must be chosen and served.

To say yes to the One who is revealed most clearly in the face of the obedient servant, Jesus Christ, means to say no at times to other claimants. It means ordering priorities.

Part of the trouble with us humans, of course, is that we always jumble our priorities. In biblical terms, the trouble with mammon is not that it is evil. The trouble is that you cannot build your life on it, because to worship it means to worry forever about it.

Mammon can be money. As American theologian, Frederick Buechner quips: "There are people who use up their entire lives making money so they can enjoy the lives they have entirely used up."

If it's your success in business, or your bank account, or your sex life, or your children; you are probably going to worry a great deal. Or, to put it another way: if you try to squeeze something infinite out of something finite, you will not only be frustrated. You will very likely squeeze the life out of it, as well.

That is the sad fact of idolatry.

This is one of the difficult lessons parents have to learn again and again. If children are expected to provide peace, happiness, contentment; the load will be too heavy for the relationship to bear. If your ego, your sense of self worth, is dependent on your child's accomplishments – as an athlete or a scholar or a professional or a social achiever – then that child is being asked to carry an enormous load, a crippling load.

So, whatever happiness is dependent upon – whether it be possessions, power, achievement – you become vulnerable, spiritually. And you cannot, then, be free. For unremitting dependency on something, which is conditional – no matter what form – becomes a kind of spiritual enslavement.

We live ultimately as recipients of a gift – the gift of life. But in our own striving, we so easily misplace it by false starts and attempts to secure it by our own devices.

That which opens a new path for us to find our way again is the One who seeks to give us a grace that accepts us in our flaws. Our inevitable touches of self-interest and related guilt. Our slippery insecurity, which leads us to try to grasp something we can control.

We are claimed by grace. And therefore, we are free; free to recognize our limits, but utilize our energies, too!

God knows that we need the sense of freedom, which comes from being loved. That allows us to escape, at least in part, from the incessant drumbeat of trying to find our validation – as human beings – through the acquisition of things or the illusion of control.

We are free to engage the world differently. In the hustle of today's world, where the pressure for success and personal aggrandizement is so unremitting, to say, "No, there is another way."

There is a way that leads home, home to life and joy and love.

- Home to a peace that the world can neither give nor ever take away.
- Home to a fellowship that death itself cannot destroy.
- Home to a security that cannot be shaken, though Heaven and Earth pass away.

For we have a God, who has never left us and who, in His love, will not leave us still.

One who, in Christ, bears a mercy which crowds out rejection. One who offers us the joy of service.

And what is this service? Nothing more than to help – in whatever way we can – other people to taste God's pardon when things go wrong. Find a nudge toward new life when things feel helpless. Discover a hint of hope when courage is lost.

Prayer: Lord, be the master of my life that I may be free and energetic in serving others.

Amen

STRUGGLING TO FIND OURSELVES

The theme that life is a journey is as old as the Odyssey and as contemporary as the 20th Century's novel, *Ship of Fools*. Movies are replete with the image: a young man journeys to the promised land of New York City to become a *Midnight Cowboy* seeking to find himself. While in *Harry and Tonto,* it is an old man who leaves home in order to complete his life.

American essayist, lecturer, and poet who led the Transcendentalist movement of the mid-19th Century, Ralph Waldo Emerson comforted those who struggle to find themselves with:

"Life is a journey, not a destination."

I invite you to take a journey, too – a journey of the spirit, to the solitary places where the settled crust of daily life can be broken open.

We begin – even if we are in the middle of our lives – by wrestling with ourselves. Who am I? Why am I here? Where am I going? What choices shall I make?

First, we must be true and honest with ourselves. Most of us are not yet complete. It may take us more than the forty days Jesus struggled in the wilderness. More by far, than forty years … but we must all struggle to find ourselves.

"To find out about ourselves is always something of a wilderness experience," wrote Lloyd John Ogilvie, in his daily devotional, *Turn Your Struggles Into Stepping Stones.* "We find ourselves when we are put to the test – when forces beyond us – place us in crisis."

Emerson went on to say:

"To be yourself in a world that is constantly trying to make you something else is the greatest accomplishment."

In a complex world, which our Father has made, there are no easy choices. To choose one thing means inevitably to reject another. What you choose to do is always tinged with a wistfulness of what you chose not.

In his classic legend of Faust, German writer and statesman Johann Wolfgang von Goethe wrote:

"Alas, our acts, as well as our sufferings, cramp the course of our lives." There is great pessimism about life. Because in a world of great terror and uncertain choices, people desire to flee responsibility and need someone to blame. "The devil made me do it."

Thus, during the height of Washington D.C.'s Watergate affair, then General Haig could speak of "sinister forces" to account for an eighteen-minute gap on the tapes of then-President Richard Nixon.

And yet, while we can speak of the banality of evil, deeds are perpetrated by seemingly ordinary people. We know that its intensity and its corrupting power is greater than simply the individual evil that lies within us. It is awesome in its cumulative power to destroy, to crush human existence. There is a mystery in evil, and the devil personifies that mystery.

There is a mystery in our freedom, too. A freedom that is somehow always anxious because it is real; even though we are finite and conditioned by historical circumstances. Evil grows out of the abuse of freedom.

That's something, which the old story of the forbidden fruit in the Garden illustrates. Is it the serpent that is most dangerous? Or the apple that is most dangerous? No. The danger does not really come to Adam and Eve from the outside.

Mankind itself is its own danger. The Promethean heart, which exploded is not set off by a charge from the outside, but from within. It is what flows out of the heart of humankind that can cause humanity to fall from grace, to die.

It is the perennial over-reaching – to believe in nothing, beyond itself. Believing in no one, becoming its own center of things, its own god. The creature tries to use its freedom to dispense with the Creator.

When that occurs – with what is humanity left – but its own philosophies and sciences and techniques? The Creator is banished, and humanity is given over to itself. But in its very moment of triumph, comes the inevitable temptation to utilize every good creative thing for destructive purpose. That out of our own creativity flows both those things that bless and those things that curse; which do violence to all that we mean by humaneness.

We human beings stand dangerously near the point where our control over nature can tempt us to take it all in our own hands – with frightening results. Foreign terrorists fly into skyscrapers with hijacked planes, home grown terrorists destroy innocent lives with the guns we've made. Our nuclear arsenals and the leaders who control them <u>can</u> destroy life and destroy the world as we know it. We live in dangerous, dangerous times.

Our capacity to program and to change may mean that individual human personality will not be able to resist manipulation, mechanization. To take our destiny into our own hands; holding no allegiance beyond ourselves, being accountable to nothing beyond ourselves does not mean freedom. Rather, we are placing ourselves under another's control.

In the gospel of Luke 4:1, he tells us that Jesus "led by the spirit" went into the wilderness to be tested by the devil. But for Jesus, there was only one supernatural will; there was <u>one</u> God. The one basic standard against which all decisions must be judged is obedience to the holy will of God.

Emerson again:

"All I have seen teaches me to trust the Creator for all I have not seen."

Most of us can review the stories, which are our lives. And we can retrace the journey we've made. We can see that the small deaths and births, intense joys and unrelieved tragedies have been milestones for us.

And they have shown us that when the smooth and settled crust of life is broken – then we come to our clearest vision of God, at work. The Center, leading and forming us into his Body, called to be a servant people, in a world where struggle is part of life.

Prayer: Dear Lord, let me remember the words of evangelist Vance Havner ... "If you are a Christian; you are not a citizen of this world trying to get to Heaven; you are a citizen of Heaven making your way through this world."

Amen

SUFFERING & GOD

In his Letter to the Romans 8:37-39, Saint Paul writes: "For I am persuaded that neither death, nor life, nor angels, nor principalities, nor powers, nor things present, nor things to come. Nor height, nor depth, nor any other creature shall be able to separate us from the love of God which is in Christ Jesus our Lord."

"Those words," said Paul Tillich, existentialist philosopher and influential theologian of the 20th Century "are among the most powerful ever written. Their sound is able to grasp human souls in desperate situations.

"In my experience," the Reverend Tillich said, "they have proven to be stronger than the sound of exploding shells, of weeping at open graves, of the sighs of the sick, the moaning of the dying. They are stronger than the self-accusation of those who are in despair about themselves, and they prevail over the permanent whisper of anxiety in the depths of our being."

This good Lutheran reverend is right. Here, we are dealing with one of the most monumental passages in all Scripture or literature. Yet, the power of these words is not derived from poetic sentiment or impressive rhetoric. No, the power of these words comes from the fact that they are wrung out of personal human experience.

When Paul writes about tribulations, distress, persecution, famine, nakedness, peril or sword – he is writing from his own life experience.

And, through these experiences, in the depth of these threatening events; Paul discovered a power greater than all other powers. A power of personal affirmation that was greater than either the anxiety of living or the fear of dying. A power greater, he said, than anything else in all creation.

"Nay, in all these things, we are more than conquerors ...."
I believe that if any one of us were to stop for a moment right now and think about our own life journey, we would become acutely aware again of just how mixed the data of life is:

> Of how good people whom we knew, perhaps came to love, became victims overnight of diseases, robbed of vitality.

> Of how people who seemed to care for absolutely nothing beyond their own drive for acquisition, gained much at the expense of others.

> Of how, in our own lives, perhaps, it was apparently mere chance, timing alone, which saved us from, or condemned us to some public shame or private humiliation.

I think it's impossible to review our own lives – let alone the lives of others – without being struck again by just how complicated, ambiguous and precarious life is. How riddled it is with injustice and marked by incoherence and suffering.

The suffering of Paul and other Christians came <u>because</u> of their faith, and they accepted that suffering for the sake of the people whom they tried to serve. And out of love for Christ. They did not seek suffering, they did not glorify it. Nor did they pretend that if one only believed enough, somehow God would take them off the hook, remove their suffering.

But what they found in their experience was something which can reach across the tragedies all human beings experience; a hidden kind of meaning. Because in light of the life, death and resurrection of Jesus Christ, they knew that even senseless suffering, even humiliating death (death on a cross, death of an innocent) can acquire meaning.

It is not a meaning that is cheaply or automatically offered. Nonetheless, it is given. And one can appropriate something of it.

Let me share with you something from a remarkable document by a young woman who was a student at Duke University. Her name was Thaniel Armistead.

As a child, she was afflicted by cystic fibrosis, a hereditary, eventually fatal disease mainly affecting the lungs. Despite a valiant fight with great pain and suffering, she died.

But at her memorial service, one of her professors read Thaniel's paper on "Tragedy and Christian Faith." She recalled the shock of discovering that moral people suffer, that tragedy isn't something that just strikes the unlucky. That life is unfair.

Thaniel had been raised to be religiously skeptical. Indeed, she called herself an atheist. But, she wrote: "One night in November, I started reading C.S. Lewis' *Miracles*.

"Halfway through the book, all my pet arguments for atheism had been shot down, and I was in great terror that God might be real. Then, I read a section, which explained who Jesus was – what the crucifixion had accomplished in overcoming sin, death and evil, once and for all.

"Interestingly, *Miracles* does not contain such a section. I have reread it several times since then and I am sure. Yet, I know what I saw; draw your own conclusions.

"John 3:16 – the only Bible verse I knew – suddenly became perfectly clear to me. 'For God so loved the world, that He gave His only begotten Son, that whosoever believeth in Him should not perish, but have everlasting life.'

"I recall thinking that if this were true, it was the most important thing that ever happened. And that this meant that the explanation and cure, the heart of the mystery all lay <u>in</u> suffering, this man's suffering and that <u>all</u> suffering thereby had meaning.

"God must know and care after all, because He was in it with us. Suddenly, there was a Presence in the room, a Person so alive that He almost made the air tingle, a Person who was utterly <u>good</u>. And so, I became a new creation in Christ Jesus."

Now, Thaniel was not relieved of her physical suffering – not at all. Nor of her intellectual struggling, nor of wrestling with doubts or making false starts. But she came to know the secret, which Paul proclaims for all of us: the amazing power of God's love. " ... if God be for us, who can be against us?" (Romans 8:31)

That love does not protect us against all suffering. Indeed, reflecting that love will always get us some sort of suffering. Because whenever you care or express concern for others, it will cost you something.

No. We are not promised immunity, protection against suffering, but rather protection in all suffering. The strong love of God, which can allow us to walk dark valleys with confidence. That beyond our frail power, there is something, which nothing in all creation can ever take from us. God's love.

Prayer: Grant us the peace, which surpasses all human understanding to keep our hearts and minds through Jesus Christ, our Lord.

Amen

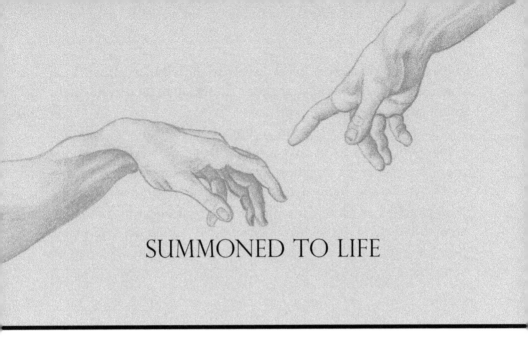

SUMMONED TO LIFE

Years ago, there was a brave man and an astute political commentator, Stewart Alsop, fighting a valiant but losing battle against cancer. He began his final magazine column with these words: "There comes a time when a dying man must die. ...."

Mr. Alsop faced his own destiny with great nobility. It is, of course, your destiny and mine, too. For we all come to an end of life, to a time when a dying man or woman must die, must relinquish all control ... to a dead end.

And for those who remain after, there is always a sense of grief. Hear LA Times columnist Jim Murray's poignant words about his wife: "This is the column I never wanted to write, the story I never wanted to live to tell. I lost my lovely, Gerry the other day. I lost the sunshine and the roses, the laughter in the other room. I lost the smile that lit up my life ... she took the magic and the summer with her."

Many read those words with eyes misted by tears. If not for Jim Murray and his beloved Gerry, then tears for ourselves and for someone we have loved and lost. As Mark Twain said: "When somebody you love dies, it's like when your house burns down. It isn't for years that you realize the full extent of your loss ...."

In the Bible, John writes of the raising of Lazarus to demonstrate that in Jesus, people are given life, summoned to life. Yet, the miracle is not described in any flamboyant way. Indeed, a great deal of the story has to do with grief. We read that Mary and Martha and the townsfolk of Bethany wept for Lazarus. And Jesus wept, too. Why?

Because, as Aristotle said, "death is a dreadful thing for it is our end." It is the cold fact of our ultimate inability to be our own source of life. Or even to control and mold and shape our own existence.

So, from the moment of our birth, we move through life strangely toward death. And there is no time in life when we are not surrounded by death.

The death that comes to loved ones and friends who die or move away or are lost. And the dying, too, of old images and assurances we counted upon, the trusted allegiances and our dependable ways of doing things.

There is a dying when old principles and cherished absolutes and holy truths no longer seem so certain. And we are unsure whether our society has exhausted the spiritual legacy of its Judaic-Christian tradition. Have we used up the well springs of compassion and fairness?

And we are even unsure, at times, about ourselves. Whether we will make it, whether we can keep some sense in the sanity and sanctity of life and not be overwhelmed. At such times, we either die and give up on life or we are summoned forth and become new people.

Loren Eiseley, the great naturalist and essayist wrote a poem about being in coyote country. Out there, alone, kneeling down to drink from a cool spring, he suddenly found his hand inches away from a coiled rattlesnake.

"He never bussed – though his sensing tongue had flickered.
As I drew back on my knees, my hand was beside his head ...
My pulse beat to no purpose
For I was distinctly dead...."

The rattlesnake, for many, is a symbol of death. The dying that surrounds and pains and troubles and hurts us. The dying that is about all the uncertainties of an always-changing world that can either destroy us. Or help us to see others and recognize ourselves in new ways. Death is either an ending or a beginning.

The Apostle Paul saw this clearly. In his letter to the Romans 6:9,14 he wrote, "Knowing that Christ being raised from the dead dieth no more; death hath no more dominion over Him. For sin shall not have dominion over you: for ye are not under the law, but under grace."

Thus, we confront the paradox: to live we must die.

In Romans 6:3-4, he writes: "Know ye not, that so many of us as were baptized into Jesus Christ were baptized into his death? Therefore we are buried with Him by baptism into death: that like as Christ was raised up from the dead by the glory of the Father, even so we also should walk in newness of life."

In Jesus Christ, God says to each one of us in effect:

Because I love you, I want you to die. Because I love you, I want you to put to death your desire to be your own god. Because I love you, I want to be your God – so that you may have new life, in me.

Dietrich Bonhoeffer, a remarkable man who was executed a few weeks before the collapse of the Nazi regime at the age of 39, once wrote: "When Christ calls a man, he bids him to come and die."

To die to what? To die to our frantic denial of death by which we try to stay in control. By which we seek to be the source of life to ourselves. To be our own god.

To die, that we might allow the Lord to mold and shape our lives. And as we do, to experience some small but significant taste of His victory over death.

It happens, you know. This dying in Christ to live anew.

Best-selling author, Keith Miller wrote about a woman named Alice who shared this story about her childhood to a group:

"'When I was a little girl, I was put in an orphanage. But as far back as I can remember, I had a longing to be adopted and loved by a family. I thought about it day and night. But everything I did seemed to go wrong. I tried too hard to please everyone who came to look me over, and all I did was drive them away. Then one day, the head of the orphanage told me a family was going to take me home. I got so excited that I started to cry. The matron told me that I was on trial. She reminded me that it might not be a permanent arrangement.

"'But I knew it would be. So I went home with this family and started school in their town. And life began to open up for me, just a little. But one day, a few months later, I came home from school and ran in the front door of the big old house we lived in. No one was at home, but there in the middle of the front hall was my battered old suitcase with my coat thrown over it. As I stood there and looked at that suitcase, it slowly dawned on me what it meant. They didn't want me. And I hadn't even suspected.'

"There was a pause. And then, Alice cleared her throat and said, almost matter-of-factly. 'That happened to me 7 times before I was 13 years old.' And then, when Alice saw that the others had tears in their eyes for her, she held up her hand and shook her head slightly. 'Don't,' she said with a genuinely happy smile. 'I needed my past. You see – it brought me to God.'"

Here is the story of a woman who experienced the reality of the death of rejection, of alienation, in a way that few of us can imagine. And yet, she is able to rejoice. Why? Because as all else failed, the One whose love proved itself on the cross called her to life with Him.

It was the love that summoned Lazarus out of the tomb. Which summons us yet to leave aside those steely feelings of self control, of anger and resentments at our betrayals and disappointments and broken dreams. Or numbness that comes when we are afraid that we can never truly belong or fit in. And let them go in renunciation for new life.

Life comes strangely not from One who offers formulas for success, self-sufficiency, and the denial of death. But One who experiences our deepest desperation, our most profound contradictions of flesh and spirit. And our most tormented ways of hurting and being hurt. And yet who – by obedience, even unto death – overcomes the power of death to separate us from the love of God.

This love has summoned others. It summons you and me still: that dying, we may live.

Prayer: If I should die before I wake, I pray the Lord my soul to take. If I should live for other days, I pray the Lord to guide my ways.

Amen

THE BLESSINGS OF LONELINESS

In their song, *Eleanor Rigby*, the Beatles sang about "All the lonely people. Where do they all come from? Where do they all belong?"

Now, when most of us hear these words, we are touched by the poignancy they express. But we really don't count ourselves among the number of truly lonely people.

For loneliness, in our common usage, connotes a kind of Eleanor Rigby existence: unfulfilled, depressed, withdrawn, unable to relate. Whereas, most of us have enough going in our lives – relationships, demands, commitments, entertainment – to exclude ourselves from that category.

Yet, not one of us can go through life without experiencing seasons of loneliness. From birth to death, separation is a strand woven into the fabric of all human experience.

And we know how difficult, how painful these periods of loneliness can be. Following in the wake of the death of a loved one, or a divorce, or a period of illness. But loneliness can strike in a fleeting, momentary fashion, too.

American theologian and author, David O. Woodyard offers a litany of such moments in his book, *Strangers and Exiles,*

Loneliness is when people ask, "How are you?" and don't wait for an answer.

Loneliness is trying to get your parents to understand how things are and feeling ashamed of your impatience with them; loneliness is struggling to accept the impatience of your children in order to listen to them.

Loneliness is going to church and being bored.

Loneliness is when you hurt someone you love.

Loneliness is making decisions that affect the lives of others and knowing you cannot avoid causing pain.

Loneliness is trite conversations.

Loneliness is holding out for moral standards when all about you, others are yielding theirs.

Loneliness is being told off by someone you never liked anyway and wishing you had done it first!"

We have all experienced these fleeting forms of loneliness, which sweep across the landscapes of our lives.

And, strangely enough, this common experience of loneliness can actually help draw us together – as brothers and sisters of the human condition. There is, in short, something very positive – contrary to our usual approach to it – about our inevitable loneliness.

First, it seems to me: loneliness can actually be the experience when we most get in touch with ourselves. Come somehow to possess ourselves at a deeper level.

Each one of us is unique. There has never been, nor will there ever be, someone exactly like you or me. Each of us is born a single entity, and dies a single entity. And in between, lives a kind of secret life of aspirations and longings – which no one else can live for us.

Loneliness reveals a good deal of our true self, which lies hidden within the more crowded house of one's life. Whenever we are separated – alone for a while – we have an opportunity to come into a kind of solemn presence with ourselves. Discover – and in a way, to create, as well – who it is that I really am.

Loneliness can offer a chance to be present to ourselves. At a deeper level, to choose the kind of self I wish to be, to change myself in some profound way.

Loneliness can be the experience when I really can listen to myself. To learn, to confront those things that may be ugly and blighted about myself – and to accept them honestly. And to encounter, too, those things that are strong and beautiful about myself – and to affirm and value them.

Our strengths, our weaknesses, our values and our ability to take possession, to take charge of our own lives: these shine through. When we are – for whatever reasons – present with ourselves. Actively present, waiting, listening. Loneliness can provide the space, the occasion, when we can get in touch with – and take hold – of ourselves.

Secondly, loneliness can provide the possibility for our deepest spiritual commitment, the possibility of faith. There is something in us, which yearns, which longs for more – more than the mere quality of existing.

We are made in such a way that we are prompted to reach out toward the indescribable. "Thou hast made us for thyself, O Lord," prayed St. Augustine, "so that our hearts are restless until they find their rest in Thee."

Loneliness can provide us with the needed prelude, which can lead to ultimate commitment, to an abiding center for our lives. In loneliness, we face the frailty of our existence. And we wrestle with the weighty questions: Is there something in which I am grounded? Is there any permanence beyond the slippery transitions of life? Is there a purpose to my existence? Is there something – or someone – to hold onto? Is there anything, which can transform my life?

We wrestle with these questions – and it is a lonely, trysting place.

But we know this. It is only by wrestling with such questions, asking them. Then the answer of God's presence with us begins to take shape, to form, to become real and personal.

Jesus did not reject the loneliness of the human condition. In the wilderness, he struggled with his own faithful understanding of vocation. Time and again, he withdraws from even his friends to renew his relationship with the One whom he taught us to call Father.

Loneliness can provide us with an opportunity to discover our deepest selves, our authentic personhood. And this experience of the soul provides the prelude for an openness to God.

Loneliness can also be the pathway to deeper relationships with other people. That sounds paradoxical.

But if loneliness is the occasion when we can most deeply get in touch with ourselves and with God, then loneliness provides the basis from which truer relationships with others can follow.

Why? Because only if you come to posses yourself, who it is you really are – and what you have to contribute – can you now give something of yourself to another. Those, who are in touch with their own depths, can reach out to touch meaningfully the depths of another.

So many people live at the level of mere contacts rather than real connections with others. So many people try to avoid solitude or loneliness as if it were a random evil. But it truly is an opportunity, a time to prepare for entering into the lives of others in a more creative manner.

For example, no person who has ever been lonely – and has used that experience to grow – can fail to be touched by the loneliness of someone else. Loneliness can become a means by which we are linked to other people. And so respond to the Lord's calling to enter compassionately into the experience and lives of other people, caringly.

Some years ago, Barbra Streisand sang a song with this refrain:"People who need people are the luckiest people in the world."

We're all the luckiest people in the world. For who among us doesn't need to belong, to be related, to be affirmed, to give and enter into the lives of others, meaningfully.

But, surprisingly, the pathway for entering into the deepest relationships in life may be in those very times when we experience loneliness. Use it creatively – and let God enter into the secret, unspoken life we each live.

Prayer: Dear Lord, help to use my moments of loneliness to find you and your purpose for me in the world.

Amen

THE CURSE OF PERFECTIONISM

Newsweek Magazine reviewed a significant work by Rutgers University historian, Philip Greven entitled *the Protestant Temperament*. Working from early American diaries, letters and sermons; Greven traces three distinctive types of child-rearing, family life and adult expectations.

Of the three kinds of temperament, which Greven describes, the most familiar one is what we would popularly refer to today as "the Puritan" or "Evangelical" model.

Obedience and submission were important religious values for that model. Life was an earnest, serious affair with the destiny of one's soul to be determined by one's conduct. One was to strive – all within one's self – for a kind of total, moral perfection.

Now, on the surface in a fairly permissive age such as ours, that may seem to be a praiseworthy kind of goal. After all, didn't the poet Robert Browning write: "A man's reach should exceed his grasp, or what's a Heaven for?"

But like any good thing taken too far, a high ideal of personal perfection can become a burden, a crippling and dehumanizing affair. A curse of perfectionism can afflict human beings. And we see it all around us.

Psychologists tell us that perfectionism is really a kind of defense mechanism. To hide behind, when we are afraid of conflict or criticism by others. Or, being afraid that something may come along which would rob us of our own good opinion of ourselves. So, many people play the perfectionism game. You know how it's played.

Buy time and space to protect yourself from your insecurities, from admitting your own limitations and weaknesses. The person, caught up in trying to be perfect, may never quite get anything finished. Because, whatever it is, it is not quite "right" enough. He or she procrastinates and just can't put the finishing touches on it. Or s/he needs more information. Or the time isn't really right for it or...whatever.

So, the perfectionist can postpone – and wait for the perfect occasion when it can be done perfectly. The book s/he means to write someday, the boat s/he means to build or the person s/he wishes to marry. S/he will just wait for the perfect time or the perfect person to come along, one fine day.

Now this kind of mechanism can afflict very talented and very able people. Folks who really do have something of value and significance to contribute to society. For example, there was a young assistant professor in the East, a brilliant man really, who just couldn't get around to finishing his doctoral dissertation. He had come close to completing it several times. But then, at the last moment, discarded it all in a fit of despair. And started over again. Why? Because, it was not perfect. A kind of paralysis set in with the fear of not covering every possible fact, every phase, every possibility in research. He feared losing control, admitting vulnerability and taking a risk.

Fear, of course, is the basic enemy of our growth as persons. Fear is what ultimately shuts us off from other people. And prevents us from tapping our strengths and using our inner resources, creatively. And while perfectionism provides a certain kind of defense against this fear – it ultimately doesn't work.

Well, that's all well and good to describe the problem. But are there any resources for breaking out of this kind of self-defeating behavior? In a *Peanuts* cartoon strip, Lucy speaks to Charlie Brown who is leaning dejectedly against a fence. She asks: "Discouraged again, eh Charlie Brown?" Then she adds: "You know what your trouble is? The whole trouble with you is that you're YOU!" And Charlie Brown asks,"Well, what in the world can I do about that?" To which Lucy replies grandly: " I don't pretend to be able to give advice ... I merely point out the trouble!"

But there is liberating news for people afflicted by perfectionism. Christian faith is designed for imperfect people ... people who recognize their limits as well as their strengths. People who are free to admit that they are not gods, but human beings. Humans, with very real needs and vulnerabilities, as well as capabilities and potential.

So, the Apostle Paul saw into the heart of this liberating news in Romans 5:8 when he wrote: "God commendeth His love toward us, in that, while we were yet sinners, Christ died for us."

And that is God's own proof of His love toward us. Christ came for imperfect people in an imperfect world. Everything that Jesus said or did had to do with freeing men and women from their bondage of self-preoccupation, self-estrangement. Releasing them from the pressure of guilt, before God, and within themselves.

He said that He had come to seek and to save, that which is lost.

He totally ignored the usual moral distinctions between "good people" and "bad people." We are all alike, in need, until we are found by the redeeming love of God. And no one is excluded. No one is too depraved or too enslaved by self-destructive patterns or too enmeshed in self-predicament to be outside His love.

The only thing that can cut us off from this liberating power of God's love and acceptance is the illusion that we really don't need it. The good news cannot be heard by those who think that they are already good enough.

That surely beckons to the person afflicted by perfectionism. For it gets tiring, after a while, manning the towers of self-defense. It's lonely inside there, where you have to pretend not to be afraid, not to hurt, not to have fear of failure or a fear of risk-taking.

The good news is that we don't have to pretend. You can accept yourself as you are. With your needs and with your fears, all because you are accepted by God as you are. We're free to be human. And not to have to posture as the utterly competent, utterly capable person; burdened with the impossibility of exceeding and excelling.

But how often this has gotten twisted around? With Christianity being hamstrung by the admonitions of a misguided Sunday school teacher who cautioned her young charges, "Now be good, children," she said, "so God will love you."

That is not gospel. It is not Christian faith. Because Christian faith is for imperfect – not perfect – people. Jesus called as his disciples his closest associates, his co-workers. Some very fallible people: Peter and Andrew, James and John – scarcely models of perfection. Not saints made out of plaster, but out of flesh and blood.

And Jesus shared his gift with these very ordinary, very untidy, very pedestrian people. Which should always be a source of encouragement to us all.

And always, He led them with a patience born out of respect for their essential personhood. He enticed and evoked and solicited the potential for good, which was in each of them.

He saw their weaknesses, yes – but also their strengths, the best in them. And encouraged that to come out.

So …

We do not have to belong to some sort of spiritual elite in order to be counted as sons and daughters of God.

We do not have to master some new esoteric vocabulary to gain admission to the company of God's people.

We do not have to strive after an impossible perfectionism in order to make ourselves worthy to have any ultimate meaning in life.

We simply have to see that we are in need. And that God, in Christ, is anxious to meet that need with his own good gifts. D.T. Niles, the great Asian Christian leader, once said that "telling the good news of Christ is simply one beggar telling another, where to find bread."

There's liberating power in this good news. For it relieves us of the burden of pretension and crippling pride and fear, inhibiting our growth and making us less than we are.

We may not always succeed – we may succumb to worry about meeting expectations. But there is One who loves us as we are – and whose presence is ever reassuring.

Bishop William Quayle, awake one night fruitlessly worrying, heard God say to him. "Quayle, you go to bed. I'll sit up the rest of the night."

Whimsically put, there's liberating news behind that. None of us is strong enough to succeed in everything. So, we are free simply to do the best that we can – and no more. Have confidence that the larger load has under it, shoulders stronger than ours and behind it, a mind wiser than ours.

Prayer: Bring out the best in me, oh Lord. And let me not wallow in perfectionism or procrastination in doing your work in the world.

Amen

THE EASTER CHOICE

Everybody loves Easter.

Merchants love it as people rush out to buy new clothes to replace old ones. Children and candy makers love it, setting up a delectable reciprocity of chocolate bunnies and cash. And everywhere, there are flowers, signifying again the renewal of the seasons, the promise of nature.

The late Theodore Gill tells of seeing an annual Easter pageant at New York's Radio City Music Hall. People -- Christians, non-Christians, anti-Christians – all burst into applause at the climax of the production as long-limbed chorus girls wave long-stemmed lilies and suddenly create a living cross.

A plus sign – is the popular Easter notion of the return of lovely spring after dreary winter. And there's the re-birth of baby chicks and bunny rabbits.

Or the more sophisticated Easter notion that goodness can't be kept down. The heroic element in human life will always live on in the memories and ideals of people. The Easter, which everybody loves, fits into our 21st Century world so comfortably.

It's the original Easter, the event of the resurrection; a very specific day in a very specific garden, which creates problems.

Somehow – almost from the beginning if we listen to Saint Paul – the resurrection of Jesus of Nazareth was an embarrassment to many people.

It still is today … and a stumbling block. A particular man who was crucified, who was dead and hastily buried, came to life again.

It's not that hard to accept Jesus as a good teacher, or as an admired man or as a hero, who remained true to his task to the very humiliating and bitter end. He deserves universal respect.

But when you get to all this other: a tumbled stone, an empty tomb, a risen person – isn't that where the Christian world-view begins to seem so shaky, to rumble with doubt? Isn't that where certainty and credibility begin to fall apart?

In the 1972 TV movie, *The Crucifixion of Jesus*, David Wolper tries to recreate the events in Jesus' life from Palm Sunday through Good Friday, using the camera much in the fashion of a contemporary news story.

The dramatic part of the documentary-style stops with the cross, then John Houston appears on the screen to continue the narrative. That is a very Biblical touch; nowhere are we offered a running-account, you-are-there picture of the Easter event.

Indeed, no one was there.

Something happened. But what? How exactly? We do not know.

What we see is that a group of men and women thought it was all over. Knowing that Jesus was dead; they are startled, frightened, then thrilled by the presence of their Lord, who could not be stopped by death itself.

They are changed by this risen One who comes with a single word in the garden, calling his earthy mother by name: "Mary ...

Such is the gospel account. And what happens to these people, these disciples? They are transformed, given courage to go out into the world, to face impossible odds and to triumph in expressing compassion and love and healing.

There are those who respond today to the Jesus who stands for generalized love, for peace and joy, for the festive spirit, a kind of freedom from conventional prudence.

They love Him for his zest, His hatred of sham, His wisdom.

But they are embarrassed -- or turned off – by the story of His rising from the dead. It may strike them as a kind of conventional happy ending tacked on by enthusiastic, credulous disciples.

They rejoice in Easter – as a sign of renewal, of human hope – but they can't believe in the resurrection of Jesus.

But without the resurrection, we would know nothing of Jesus at all. It isn't a sort of postscript added to the Gospels. Every line of the New Testament was written by people who were convinced that God had raised his Son from the dead.

In that faith they lived – and in that faith, many of them died.

There is a choice involved in Easter Day. Either this man, Jesus, was on the side of life; who loved as no other person has ever quite loved; who healed and restored people; who lifted them up out of the places of despair; who forgave; who rejoiced in the One, He called Father. Either, He himself was crushed at an early age and died a cruel and meaningless death. Or God affirmed the ultimate triumph of such a life by raising Him from the dead.

It is a choice. It has always been a choice.

You can confront it by saying: it's too good to be true. I just don't believe it. Or, that people just made it up because they were afraid, themselves, to die.

If you do, then you choose to live in a world where a noble man like Jesus may be crushed and crucified by evil. And that is simply the end. Then you choose to live in a world whose final lord and master is death. Where goodness and laughter and joy have no ultimate echo in the heavens.

Or, somewhere deep down within you a voice says: "Yes."

Perhaps, the voice is very faint, perhaps it is only able to whisper: "Lord, I believe; help my unbelief."

But, if you allow it to speak – however tentatively, however wistfully – you may find the voice beginning to strengthen. You begin to sing a new song; a song of transforming power – of affirmation and hope. It's a song, which will grow and swell and resonate through your life. A song of deep joy, which you will gladly sing with others. Knowing that your life is held in a love, which you can trust, even at the hour of your own death.

In a world grown weary of people who say no to the yearnings, the deep longings, the aspirations of the human soul for an abundant and meaningful life; God waits for your answer – for your "yes" to the victory of Christ Jesus. No matter how clear – or how fragile – your "yes" may be.

When you say it, there will be a real Easter celebration in your life. And Easter will triumph over all the Good Fridays that you, too, may encounter.

Prayer: Lord, I believe; help my unbelief. Let me say "yes" to life, to receive God's abiding gift, and to join in the real celebration of Easter.

Amen

THE GREAT INVITATION

One of the greatest invitations of all time was given by Jesus when he said in Matthew 11:28, "Come unto me, all ye that labour and are heavy laden, and I will give you rest."

To whom is he speaking, really? In the context of St. Matthew's gospel, the reference is clear enough: to all those people in his day who found religion to be a heavy load and burden; those who labored under an elaborate system of religious law and scruples.

The teachers and scribes of those days proudly referred to their religion as a "yoke of the law." To which one must submit in order to find true validation for personal existence, true meaning and purpose.

It was a comprehensive code – with a whole card index of laws. It was designed to cover every imaginable human activity, throughout life … from cradle to grave.

Yet, we are a far different kind of society – pluralistic, industrial, mobile. A far cry from Palestine of twenty centuries ago, when Jesus issued His invitation.

In what sense, then, can these words of His speak to us today?

German-born Lutheran theologian and existentialist philosopher, Paul Tillich, once wrote a powerful sermon on this text and entitled it "The Yoke of Religion." In it, he said, that whatever our situation in life, we are nonetheless all burdened and heavy laden. Listen to his words:

"All human beings are sighing under the law, a law which is religion and a religion which is law. We labor and toil because we are beings who know about finitude, limits and boundaries; about our impermanence, about the danger of living, and about the tragic character of existence.

"Fear and anxiety are the heritage of all people, as the Apostle Paul knew when he looked at the Jews and the pagans. Restlessness drives us during our whole lives, as Augustine knew. A hidden element of despair is in each of our souls as the great Danish Protestant, Søren Kierkegaard, knew. 'There is no religious genius, no keen observer of the abyss of the human soul; nobody capable of listening to the sounds of his heart, who would not witness to this insight into human nature and existence.'

"Splits and gaps are in every soul. For instance, we know that we are more than dust; and yet we know also that we are going to be dust. We know that we belong to a higher order than that of our animal needs and desires; and yet, we know that we shall abuse the higher order in the service of our lower nature. We know that we are only small members of the spiritual world; and yet, we know that we shall aspire to the whole, making ourselves the center of the world.

"This is man; and because this is man, there is religion and law. The law of religion is a great attempt of man to overcome his anxiety and restlessness and despair. To close the gap within ourselves, and to reach immortality, spirituality and perfection. So, we labor and toil under religious law in thought and act."

Current religious movements offer a clearly defined belief system along with specific demands for performance and explicit taboos as well. If you are a believer – a true believer—then, you must accept this system. And conform to the requirements if you are to find salvation from the anxiety, despair and sense of death, which (according to Pastor Tillich) touch us all.

But suppose that one fine day, while still counting yourself a true believer, you begin to doubt some idea or another in this system. Something doesn't seem quite right when measured against your own experience – some teaching or requirement or prohibition.

Suppose then you begin to labor and toil under a demand to try to affirm things; which you have begun, however hesitantly, to question. Or suppose that you finally decide to escape the whole scene – to reject all formal religion and live as a thorough skeptic.

Do you then escape from the burden of religion? I don't think so. For human nature cannot live in the emptiness of more skepticism; cannot live in a vacuum.

The son of famous and aggressive atheists recanted his parent's dogmatism. Because he found, as a young man, that atheism is a completely negative philosophy and a person has to have something more. Which is only confirmation for recognizing our need as human beings for some kind of framework, for making sense out of our existence and experiences -- for meaning.

And one can never find meaning without some act of faith.

The question is, then: can we find a kind of faith that lets us <u>be</u> as human beings? Which helps us affirm ourselves and others, and yet which equips us to deal with the dark forces which do contend against us?

There are plenty of faiths competing for allegiance. Religious yokes can be found in places which one would least expect to look. In political ideologies which can be advocated with religious fanaticism and zealotry. Or in scientific theories which can be defended with religious dogmatism. Or in utopian schemes, which promise instant wholeness for persons and societies. And which can be proclaimed by their devotees with religious fervor.

Somehow, there is no escaping the yoke; the heavy burden of trying to find some strategy for dealing with anxiety and despair. Those things, which Pastor Tillich says, lead to the rise of religion and law.

Then, consider afresh the words of Jesus: " Come unto me ...."

In Matthew 11: 29-30, Jesus goes on to say: "Take my yoke upon you, and learn of me ... and you shall find rest unto your souls. For my yoke is easy and my burden is light."

I think that this passage tells us a great deal about life and its ordering. Jesus speaks to all those who are aware of their defeat as human beings by those forces which attempt to wring human validation from conformity.

Jesus invites – does not command – us to find a center for life in which we can <u>be</u> as human beings. In Him, we can find a center around which we can order our existence.

Love is that center – and motivating power. It is a center around which we can recognize our human dilemma; and yet, celebrate too, the uniqueness of our own personhood and the gift of hope.

It is the centering movement in which we are embraced by the love of God. A love, which does not wait until we have conformed to some dicta or other before seeking us out. But a love which embraces us as we are; in all our contradictions and ambiguities and false starts. And loves us nonetheless.

Such love liberates us to love God and ourselves. And from that love, our neighbor, and our world. It is the centering movement that enables us to begin our life again in a new way.

We point not to our own excellence, but to the excellence of the Lord of life; who comes in our daily struggle with anxiety, death and despair.

He calls us to His side with the promise of relief from the strain and anxiety of trying to obey impossible laws. Some biblical translators use the word "relief" rather than "rest." It suggests something of an intolerable burden being lifted from us – allowing us to run, or climb or dance or live with a certain free abandon and joy. The power of life within us is set free to express ourselves in original creative thought and action; our hearts are uplifted; our minds opened and free.

Prayer: Lord, help me order my life with your love at the center and the freedom to climb and dance and live with joyous abandon.

Amen

THE HEART IN EXILE

Those of you who have seen the motion picture *"E.T. - The Extra Terrestrial"* will have no difficulty recalling the terror felt by the little alien creature. As it is left behind in the dark woods; as its fellow creatures flee aboard their spacecraft from the menacing, faceless men and machines who seek them out.

Who can forget the piercing screech of abandonment, deeper than any language can convey. And the palpitating glow of fear, which springs from his being?

In an instant, E.T. has become an exile. Uprooted from his environment; stripped of all support systems; cut off from all those familiar symbols and relationships which give security, meaning and order to life. All that is familiar now vanishes; all that sustains is gone; now he must dwell in a land that is not his own, a place full of threat and danger.

So it has always been for exiles: for those who have been brutally forced from their homes.

Our 20th and 21st Centuries are unparalleled in all history as a time of exiles – when millions upon millions upon millions of people have been forcibly uprooted, victimized. And the beat of suffering goes on – with the rapacious massacre of civilian people, including mothers and babies, in refugee camps around the world.

To become an exile is to become vulnerable. Not only to external forces. But to the inevitable human feelings of guilt and doubt, grief and anger, which accompany this cataclysmic event in which one's life story is shattered.

To become an exile is to be exposed directly to the brutality and evil, which is deeply embedded in the human condition. Back in the Great Depression of the 1930's, millions of Americans became exiles in their own country, too. Millions of men of all ages rode the rails; running from nothing behind, hoping for something ahead, looking for someplace to be.

Loren Eiseley was one such young exile. In his autobiography, *All the Strange Hours*, he tells of having survived a savage attack by a brakeman, while riding on a freight train. An unnamed companion asked him about his swollen and bruised face, as they shared food together.

"Around the fire," wrote Eisley, "the man looked at me with the eyes of middle-age: prison eyes, black, impenetrable, self-sufficient. He stood up in the firelight and cast the empty sack onto the flames. The paper flared briefly, accentuating the hard contours of his face.

"'Remember this,' he said suddenly, dispassionately, as though the voice originated over his shoulder. 'Just get this straight. It's all there is – and after awhile you'll see for yourself.' He studied me again without expression.

"'The capitalists beat men into line. Okay? The communists beat men into line. Right again?'

"I reckon," I ventured, more to fill in the silence growing around us than because I understood.

"He pointed gently at my swollen face. 'Men beat men, that's all. That's all there is. Remember it, kid. Take care of yourself.' He walked away then, up the dark, diverging track."

Men beat men ... that's all there is.

For this man – this exile – faith, hope and love were not the great realities of life. No, in this jungle, there was only one reality – survival. Men beat men ... that's all there is.

It was a wrenching view. Borne, no doubt, out of his own, bitter experience. And I think such an attitude is understandable, indeed given the circumstances, reasonable.

But the miracle is always when the victimized exile does not succumb to such a nihilistic, meaningless view of life. But opts for something more. Something, which will permit the affirmation of healing rather than destruction, compassion rather than narrow self-protection.

In the Bible, Isaiah experienced the agony of exile, as well. He had been forced, as a prisoner of the Babylonians, to march through the rough, flesh-tearing wilderness. To endure its unremitting heat, its scorching blast.

And when he had finally arrived at the refugee camp in Babylon, he was confined, forced to work and labor, treated as a defeated person in the ranks of failures; an object of sport and humiliation by his captors.

The scene is starkly contemporary. What did he do? Weep? No doubt. But curse God and die? No.

Isaiah believed that there was a way that lead to the fulfillment of life's potential; a way that God had made. A way that ran through the trackless wilderness. A way that was safe from the hungry wolves and moral sickness. A way for pilgrams – not for invading armies. A way of peace. The way home.

The miracle is that this shadow of a man saw it. He saw reality through the mist of insanity. And he was not mad.

The poet is prophetic. He does not succumb to the belief that life is meaningless. Rather, in Isaiah 35:4: "Say to them that are of a fearful heart. 'Be strong, fear not: behold, your God will come with vengeance … He will come and save you.'"

This is not unlike a situation faced by Martin Luther King, Jr. in the fall of 1956. The Black protestors refused to board buses where they were routinely shunted to the back and treated like second-class persons. The Montgomery, Alabama police tried to intimidate them, as a consequence of this bid for dignity.

The establishment was determined to win. The mayor instructed the city attorneys to file proceedings against the leaders of Black resisters to stop the operation of car pools, a successful part of the boycott. The cause, which Martin Luther King, Jr. championed, seemed doomed to certain failure.

He, then, preached a sermon: "The greatest of all virtues is love. Here we find the true meaning of the Christian faith and the cross. Calvary is a telescope through which we look into the long vista of eternity and see the love of God breaking forth into time."

Both the poet writing in Isaiah and young preacher speaking centuries later confronted the reality of evil in their lives and knew the scars of oppression. But they did not succumb to the view that, ultimately, nothing mattered because a stony indifference was the order of life. They refused the temptation to be cynical and pessimistic.

No. In the worst of times, in exile, they had a vision of transforming possibilities, of reversals. And they did so, because they were convinced that there is operating in human affairs; a power, which quietly works to affirm life. Even, in the midst of all which would demean and destroy it.

That power, of course, is not self-evident. It certainly cannot be recognized by the proud and arrogant, who could not conceive of its existence. Nor, perhaps, by the embittered who have come to accept inhumanity as "all there is."

Yet, even in unlikely places, there emerges a glimpse of possibility.

Indeed, the young exile, Loren Eiseley went on to become a celebrated anthropologist, educator, philosopher and naturalist. Of Eiseley, Pulitzer Prize winner Ray Bradbury wrote: "Eiseley is every writer's writer, and every human's human. . . one of us, yet most uncommon.. ."

Eiseley was never what you would call an orthodox believer. Yet, he kept encountering something other – something greater than a mere mechanistic or mechanical view of nature.

He wrote: "I am an evolutionist. I believe my great backyard Spheges (wasps) have evolved like other creatures. But watching them in the October light as one circles my head in curiosity, I can only repeat my dictum softly. In the world, there is nothing to explain the hunger of the elements to become life. There is nothing to explain why the stolid realm of rock and soil and mineral should diversify itself into beauty, terror and uncertainty. To bring organic novelty into existence; to create pain, injustice and joy demands more than we can discern in the nature that we analyze so completely.… In the world, there is nothing below a certain depth that is truly explanatory. It is, as if, matter dreamed and muttered in its sleep. But why and for what reason it dreams, there is no evidence."

Perhaps not. The mystery is that which German Lutheran theologian, Rudolf Otto called the *numinous,* the deep center of life which cannot be explained.

Is that center <u>for</u> us – or indifferent <u>to</u> us? Aware of us in our deep needs; or blind to our struggles for wholeness? Questions we confront again and again; in our life journeys, our checkered experiences.

There are times when we may be inclined to answer one way – or the other; times when we have to confess that we simply do not know.

But, then, we encounter those old stories, which were borne out of human exile and despair. A young poet and refugee, but nonetheless saying; Be strong for there is a power which strives to come to us and to save us …. And there was.

The power, which the prophet Isaiah foretold. And the power glimpsed in the face of Jesus is that power which seeks humankind's good. A power which is <u>for</u> us – and <u>not against</u> us. A power, which seeks to restore those, whose capacities for life are impaired. Who seeks to liberate those, who are oppressed and those, burdened and heavily laden.

And that, of course, means all of us at some level, at some time or other. Life involves both coherence and incoherence –- which means none of us ever arrives, ever is totally integrated and self-sufficient. None of us is ever, for example, more than a breath away from death.

And few of us are more than a paycheck from poverty. We're vulnerable to terrorists who've hijacked an airplane or some citizen armed with an AK47 in a church or a nightclub or an elementary or high school. Or a stray virus, which suddenly can lay low the strongest among us.

To some extent, all of us are exiles at times – from wholeness, from holiness, from awareness, from relationships. But in Jesus Christ, we see One who enters into our human condition to restore, to renew, to bring hope and light. Even into the darkest and most fearful places where we may find ourselves.

That is the power upon which human hope can be built.

Prayer: Dear Lord, find me in my exile, a refugee and rescue me from even my self-imposed imprisonment.

Amen

THE LORD IS MY SHEPHERD

If there is one psalm – one ancient Hebrew hymn – that is known and cherished equally by those who are steeped in Scripture and those who do not know the Bible at all – it is the Twenty-third Psalm.

All who read it -- whatever your age or your experience – find in its beautiful phrases a range and depth of insight, which satisfies and nurtures the soul. This song of praise begins and ends with simple, grateful acknowledgement of the never-failing goodness of the Lord.

I find it remarkable that these words – written thousands of years ago – still have such extraordinary power to touch people deeply. The words themselves stay so readily in our memories. As a pastor, I know how many times, for example, at some bed of pain; a person, in need, will join spontaneously in saying these words with me. And find a sense of peace.

There's a reason for its endurance, for its staying power. And that reason is that it pictures life as deeply as life is experienced. A young child, learning the psalm for the first time, once began: "The Lord is my Shepherd, that's all I want." He really wasn't very far from the heart of the matter.

Perhaps, there have been times when you, too, have found phrases of that psalm coming back to you. Perhaps, at some moment of stress or vulnerability and need; when you've encountered again the limits of your own inner resources.

Let's now focus briefly on one theme from this magnificent poem, Psalm 23:2-3: "He maketh me to lie down … He restoreth my soul."

The stanzas belong together. Because there are few of us who can have our inner strength restored; until we have been brought to that place where we must "lie down." And rest in a greater strength than our own.

Now, I know, that sounds strange and paradoxical. But then, life is a strange and paradoxical affair, too. Life, for any of us, is not a tidy, sequential kind of business. It is dynamic, ever changing, and somehow mysterious.

The paradox is this:

Until life itself compels us to come to the end of our own busy-ness with the superficial and routine,

Until we are forced to stop; to confront ourselves as we really are, to assess both our strengths and our weaknesses,

Until we get in touch with the mysterious depths of our existence, which we very often try to avoid and seldom explore ...

Then there is little likelihood of our seriously turning to the mysterious Other. To the One, whom the psalmist calls Lord. Who indeed wishes to be our shepherd and companion and guide in life's journey.

"He maketh me to lie down ..." poet and playwright W. H. Auden pointed to this paradox when he wrote; "It is where we are wounded that He speaks to us."

The extremity of our human condition, where we must lie down. Where we can no longer control everything that happens to us. Can become the occasion and opportunity to receive power and strength, beyond ourselves; to be restored.

The truth of the psalm is the truth of human experience. Dr. Douglas Steere, a devout Quaker and philosopher, cites the case history of a man of intense spiritual power. Where this truth became clear, who was made "to lie down...." Only to discover that, in his powerlessness, there came a new power; and a deeper growth toward wholeness and healing.

Here, was a man who had become a symbol of his nation's resistance to totalitarian power. The summer of 1945 was the time of Norway's celebration of liberation, from the occupation of the Nazis. All during the occupation, Bishop Berggrav, the Bishop of Oslo, had remained under house arrest. In "protective custody," because he refused to subscribe to the idolatrous claims of the Quisling regime.

In the absence of the king, Bishop Berggrav became, for Norwegians, the very symbol of resistance. With the ending of the war, there was a great outcry for the Norwegian parliament to restore capital punishment, which had been abolished previously. People demanded revenge, wanting to execute those collaborators and traitors who had betrayed their homeland. But Bishop Berggrav – as a Christian – publically resisted this emotional wave of revenge and bitterness that swept his country.

The result? He lost the public's esteem. The person who had been hailed as hero, now became the object of all kinds of public and private vilification.

One day, an American visitor sought him out to tell him that some of his fellow Christians, at least, knew what he was going through. Knew how rough things were; and yet had confidence in him for his efforts to literally love his enemies. The bishop smiled in a tired, but strangely luminous way. And he said: "You know, whenever my head gets too high above the water, God has a way of pushing me under again – and it is good."

The bishop had been brought low -- made to lie down – and yet, in the isolated depths, discovered again the goodness and trustworthiness of God.

"He maketh me to lie down … He restoreth my soul."

Well, few of us are heroic figures. But I suspect that each of us could add our own dramatic instances, where we have been brought low. Made to lie down, to confront ourselves as we are, in moments of powerlessness.

I think of a student, for instance: bright, alert, capable of success, but suddenly losing interest in what he has been programmed to do. He begins to find things are going sour; putting in his time, going through the motions; but somehow the old passion is gone. Something fearful is happening and he doesn't know quite what to do about it.

A parent, who sees the confusion of a teen-aged child; knows the kinds of destructive experimentation going on and sees a drift toward danger. And yet, knows that special quality of pain which comes from a sense of powerlessness; a bewilderment of how to get through, how to help the child redirect her life.

A partner in a relationship – who discovers that the other one upon whom so much of life has been focused, has failed in some very basic way. Who now experiences the deep hurt of a memory, which will not simply fade away. And who wonders whether the shattered pieces can ever be put back together again.

"He maketh me to lie down ..."

Yet, it is in this act of lying down, of letting go, of confronting our limits to control everything; that we are led, strangely, to that place where we can be restored. Where we can discover again our human need; and where we find One who is on our side. One who wishes to strengthen us, and relieve us of the burden of loneliness. And accompany us with His power as a shepherd cares for his sheep.

When we are made to lie down in the unfolding of life; we are, if only we accept it, confronting a great opportunity.

For then, when the easy assumptions of the surface-self are shattered. When we doubt most our own strengths and confront our own weaknesses. We are able to peek into – not an abyss – but to the very heart of God. He seeks always to grant us a re-birth, wishes to become a partner in a fresh regrouping of our resources. A power to give us focus again – and compassion for the journey ahead.

There is such an experience as spiritually dying in order to be spiritually reborn. In those moments when we are made to lie down ... we are made open to restoration.

Jesus, you know, calls himself the good shepherd; who will not abandon his sheep like some common hireling. He says of himself in John 10:17: "I lay down my life that I might take it again."

The good news of the gospel is that He laid down his life willingly -- precisely for your sake and mine. And that beyond the Good Fridays of our lives, He brings us new Easter Mornings.

"He maketh me to lie down ... He restoreth my soul."

Prayer: The Lord is my Shepherd, I shall not want.

Amen

THE MASKS WE WEAR &
THE ROLES WE PLAY

In 1969, Jesuit priest John Powell wrote a little book entitled *Why Am I Afraid To Tell You Who I Am?* He answered the question in that title by quoting a person who had said: "I am afraid to tell you who I am; because if I tell you who I am, you may not like who I am, and it's all that I have."

The thesis is that in order for a person to be truly human and fully functioning; he or she must overcome that fear and must let other people discover who he or she really is. In short, by allowing our external lives to reflect accurately what we are feeling inside.

It would seem that most of us lead "double lives," with the outside being very different from the inside and our public lives being very different from our private lives.

This doesn't mean that we are schizophrenic – split personalities. But rather as we live our lives, we do play different "parts" and different "roles." Very much like actresses and actors playing roles in a movie. In ancient Greek theater, those who acted on the stage held up different masks in order to indicate different roles or moods.

Interestingly, these masks were called "persona" – and that's where we derive our very word for "person." Mask wearing and personhood are, thus, intimately linked. That same experience of acting out roles and holding up masks is at the root of another ancient Greek word – the word for hypocrite – an actor, someone who plays a part.

The truth of the matter seems to be that to be a person, a human being, has always meant to wear a variety of masks and play various roles. There is something intrinsically positive, then, to be said about this. We all seem to need masks and roles in order to be ourselves. And this very linkage between being a person, a human being, and role-playing ought to serve as a corrective to one of the most over-worn popular dogmas of our time. Namely, the incessant call: "let it all hang out," take off our masks, expose ourselves ruthlessly and totally in all circumstances.

This is one of the rallying cries of the sensitivity movement; be gutsy, be real, take off your mask and join the party – we are told. That usually consists of letting everybody know what you really feel about them and everything else, telling others how much you dislike yourself or them.

But any real sensitivity in human relationships dictates that there are times and occasions when we should keep our masks on – and our feelings firmly in place. Not because they are phony cover-ups, but because sometimes they are the better side of ourselves. The side that is revealed when the pressure is on and the stakes are high.

There are many occasions when we must keep our feelings under control, for our own sakes as well as for the sake of those around us. If we let go with a primal burst every time we are frustrated, tripped up by another, or hurt by something or someone in life; we will simply self-destruct.

Maintaining ourselves is important for our own stability and growth; and it is also important for others. A mother, for example, goes into the sick room of a child, who is seriously ill. She wears the mask of calm and confidence, although inwardly, she is feeling helpless and anxious.

And she does this to help the child, playing a heroic part for his sake.

So, masks and roles are a necessary part of the human experience. And yet, at the same time, they can be harmful to a person's self-image. For we are always <u>more</u> than whatever masks we wear. We are always <u>more</u> than whatever roles we play. We are the sum of more than the parts.

There is a mystery about ourselves, something elusive which is nonetheless essential to our existence. And we are more complex than any of the signals we pick up which tell us how to play our various roles in life. The signals come strongly from a variety of sources in society: from home and family, church and employer, friends, the image-makers in all the various public media.

Think, for example, of the stereotypes of vocational roles. The business executive must play the role of the energetic, driving, get-up-and-go creative person. The scientist must be detached and impersonal. The policeman must be tough and self-reliant. Bartenders and barbers must be good listeners. And counselors and clergy must be pious.

The list is endless. There are well-defined role expectations; various kinds of appropriate masks which must be worn.

The trouble occurs when people play the roles so consistently that they begin to believe that they are simply what they appear to be. People get into trouble when we cannot distinguish our real selves from our masks. When, we begin to say in effect; "I am my mask, I am only a role, I am always a role." When we cannot distinguish our multi-dimensional, rich, complex and mysterious selves from the scripts we are given to play or the roles we choose to perform.

A person's spiritual life is very much tied up in this dilemma; of accepting the wider self beyond the various roles we play. Like every character in Scripture about whom we glimpse anything at all, we are simply never that consistent. We live with ambiguities and contradictions. We are a compendium of both strengths and weaknesses. We are capable of great thoughts and transcendent actions. But we are also those who hurt and need; those who are afraid and those who operate from narrow self-interest.

The question is – can we accept our humanity or not?

For example, am I a person who loses my temper sometimes and behaves irrationally. If I can admit this to myself, then I do not need to deny it by putting on a mask of placidity? And pretend that I am always calm, rational, in control.

Or am I a person who sometimes gets to feeling overwhelmed by things; so much so that I would like just to walk away from it all? If I can accept that, then I don't need to deny it by putting on a mask of serene assurance. And pretend that I am always confident and self-sufficient.

Or am I a person who can admit to the coming and going of doubts and questions. Of experiencing the dark nights of the soul; and living through dry spells in my faith and trust? If I can accept that I am such a person, then I don't have to wear the mask of pious certitude. And pretend always solid, confidence in faith, strong and courageous.

It gets pretty lonely behind the masks we wear. It's hard work to keep up the pretense that we are simply whatever role we are playing; whatever mask we are wearing for whatever reason.

But we can be of good cheer! The good news – the gospel – is that God accepts us as we are: in our strengths and weaknesses, in our victories and defeats, in our promise and in our despair.

And that nothing -- nothing that we can do -- can change His persistent, tenacious love; which beckons us to accept ourselves as we are. To wear, indeed, our masks and to play our various roles, yes. But to know all the while that they are simply masks and roles and that we are greater than these. And that we are free from the tyranny of trying to be something other than whom we really are.

Prayer: Dear God, thank you for knowing all of me and loving me anyway.

Amen

THE MEANING OF FAITH

On September 12, 1940 – as most of the world's attention was focused on the Battle of Britain and the German occupation of France; four boys set out from a village in Southern France to hunt for buried treasure.

Now, in many ways, their venture was not unusual, even in wartime. For boys are always seeking adventure as Mark Twain's 1876 novel, *Tom Sawyer* demonstrated long ago.

Legend had it that near a decaying old farmhouse on a tract of land known as Lascaux, enormous riches had been hidden underground. So, the boys commenced digging. And dug their way through an old hole in the ground, into a cave where walls were covered with some of the oldest and most beautiful prehistoric art ever found.

The art was not primitive, but highly advanced. Today, scientists marvel at the skill displayed by the unknown artists. For they demonstrated a control of color, line, shadow and methods of depicting perspective, which were lost after prehistoric times and not rediscovered until the Renaissance.

The Lascaux Cave paintings reflect what appear to have been the attempts of prehistoric man to grapple with the nature of life, the notion of a supreme being, the role of man and the things around him.

Here were men and women in the dim mists of emerging humanity. We can only guess at their circumstances, tens of thousand of years ago.

Why did they take time off from their serious business of day-to-day survival in order to create such glorious works of art? Why did they do it?

Not for profit in a society without wealth. Not for display, for the paintings are tucked away in remote corners and ceilings of caves where few would venture. Not for religious impulses in a narrow understanding of the word, for the scenes are of various animals and the hunt. And yet – precisely in those free-flowing forms of ancient animals – there is a profound religious dimension.

Christian philosopher and theologian Paul Tillich reminded us time and again that art and religion are always likened. They both are people's response to the world, which they experience. And the two are always bearers of mankind's struggle to encompass and make meaningful that experience.

For example, someone has suggested that no doubt primitive man encountered the great animals as both a blessing of food (for survival) and a bane (of threat and competition.)

To face a beast with only a stone axe or a club was one thing; but to face it when painted on the wall of a cave was another. That way, you could gain some distance from the beast; you could observe it, objectify it – reduce its terror to manageable dimensions.

Those of you who have seen the great cathedrals built in the Middle Ages know that the stone masons could take all of the terrifying forces which inhabited those dark ages; and transform them into stone images of gargoyles and the like. Frozen in stone, they could not harm.

Perhaps, editorial cartoonists serve the same function in the daily press. They can transform dictators or tyrants into caricatures -- and help us laugh at their pretensions and postures.

The late anthropologist Margaret Mead quoted a 15-year-old Texas boy as saying: "We see the world as a huge rumble as it swiftly goes by with wars, poverty, prejudice and the lack of understanding among people and nations. Then we stop and think; there must be a better way and we have to find it."

There must be a better way and we have to find it. He expressed again the belief that lurks implicitly in the cave at Lascaux; the world is somehow understandable and life is somehow manageable.

Why should the boy come to such a conclusion – a child of the

20th Century; a century of horror and excess of violence and cruelty? He stops and thinks -- and hopes.

Why should the prehistoric artist, knowing full well the tremendous forces which daily threaten his existence, go into a cave and paint them? Thus, making a statement of hope for order in the midst of chaos?

Both of them – the young man of the 20th Century and the primitive artists – face the reality of the present. And, nonetheless, hope for a way of transcending it in favor of a positive future. Both operate from faith.

The venture of faith is a theme as old as humankind and runs throughout the Bible. Abraham leaves Ur of the Chaldees in search of a new homeland, which God will show to him. Moses leads his people out of the chains of bondage into the wilderness toward a promised land. Jesus, in three short years of ministry, sets a pattern of spiritual obedience and growth that changes human consciousness forever.

It is this religious dimension of life – which asserts a better way – that makes life manageable. For example, all of us are confronted by the question; whether or not life has meaning, congruency, purpose, beauty, or rationality. That is, whether life, or being, is gracious or not.

There is plenty of evidence that it is not. It often appears that life is not gracious, but is dominated by suffering, tragedy, cruelty, insanity, irrationality and death. Yet, on the other hand, we <u>have</u> seen beauty, we <u>have</u> experienced goodness, we <u>have</u> tasted love, and <u>have</u> known faithfulness and something in us wants to hope.

The data are mixed, but we must make a response. That's the religious dimension of living. How we choose makes a difference on how we see life -- our own and the lives of other people.

We are summoned to make a response – either for or against the graciousness of being. We are called upon to make a leap of faith.

The artist in the cave made this leap; so did the young boy in Texas. The witness of the Biblical writers – and the heroes of faith whom they portray – is that yes! We are free to make this leap of trust, for the cosmos has been created by God. He has pronounced it good; and order, form, coherence, purpose, meaning can yet be affirmed and found.

Thus, Albert Einstein, the most influential physicist of the 20th Century, did his work in a culture permeated with this belief. And could make the statement that "God does not play dice with the universe."

Now faith is not only a matter of <u>seeing</u> life from a positive perspective, it also means <u>acting </u>in life in a particular way. No matter what your condition, you've been given something of great value. You are a human being, capable of reflecting upon, of responding to the world; of interpreting your experience and making a difference. You are capable of adventurous faith.

When we act and live in commitment. In a stance of faith toward the vision of Another One, we begin to experience new enrichment in life. We begin to find that new forms of relationship open up. New friendships are made, new attitudes come into our lives; replacing some of the self-negating, self-defeating attitudes so common to us all.

This kind of faith is active – and it is a better way. For it allows us to confront our world and ourselves in this knowledge. God himself loves us as we are, accepts us as we are, values us as His own. And calls us to share this acceptance, this love with others – and with the world.

We are not simply nameless little creatures in the cosmos. No. We are named by God, counted as one of his children – known and loved. We are valued and sought by the Infinite One – who in Jesus Christ comes to seek and to find us!

Prayer: Dear Lord, let me contribute beauty, goodness, love and faithfulness amidst the chaos of the world.

Amen

THE PERSUASIVE SIGN

Each one of us is distinct from any other human being.

In all of history, there has never been anyone such as you – or me. Nor shall there ever be again. There is a marvelous, irreducible, individuality, which runs through all human life.

And yet, when we begin to tell each other our own, unique, personal stories, when we share our own individual perception and life experiences; we discover that somehow we are linked in very basic, very compelling ways.

There is a commonality in life, which is as marvelous as our individuality.

This is a very personal story. But, I believe that in some ways, it is your story and my story, too. It is a story, which come from the life of one of the most illustrious persons in American theatre, Moss Hart.

As a child, Moss grew up in the obscurity of the very poor. His father was unable to find a job. The sole means by which the family supported itself was through renting rooms in their old house, in one of New York's dingiest neighborhoods.

Among the boarders was Aunt Kate – eccentric, irascible, a somewhat impossible person with whom to get along.

Yet to Moss and his brothers, Aunt Kate was nonetheless a very bright spot in an otherwise unhappy home. For somehow, from her meager monthly income, Aunt Kate managed to find enough now and then to buy the boys a book. Or, even more marvelously, she treated them to tickets for a Broadway play.

For 10-year-old Moss and his brothers, Aunt Kate was the window opening to a wider world beyond the drab walls of a deprived existence. And on Christmas, it was Aunt Kate -- and Aunt Kate alone -- who always bought a tree and presents.

But then, a tragedy occurred. And Kate – in one of her more difficult moments – crossed Moss' father once too often. The father became very angry – angry enough to order Aunt Kate to pack her things and leave his house, at once.

It was a serious break and rupture in the family. And when Aunt Kate left in a huff, she left behind a desolate little boy.

Moss was furious with his father; how could his father do such a thing? Now there would be no presents, no tree at Christmastime! Didn't his father understand that? Didn't he care?

In his grief, Moss thought he could never forgive, nor ever really love his father again.

It was Christmas Eve. Now, I'll let Moss tell the story in his own words:

"My father was very silent during the evening meal. Then he surprised and startled me by turning to me and saying: 'Let's take a walk.'

"I was even more surprised when he said, as we left the house, "Let's go down to 149th Street and Westchester Avenue.

"My heart leapt within me. That was the section where all the big stores were. Where at Christmastime, open pushcarts full of toys stood backed end-to-end for blocks on a stretch.

"On other Christmas Eves, I had often gone there with Aunt Kate. My father had known of this, of course. And I joyously concluded that this walk could only mean one thing; he was going to buy me a Christmas present.

"I <u>needed</u> some sign from my father or mother that they knew what I was going through and cared for me as much as my Aunt Kate did.

"Tugging at my father's coat, I started down the line of pushcarts. There were all kinds of things that I wanted. But since nothing had been said by my father about buying a present, I would merely pause before a pushcart to say – with as much control as I could muster – 'Look at that chemistry set!' or, 'There's a stamp album,' or 'Look at the printing press!'

"Each time, my father would pause and ask the pushcart man the price. Then, without a word, we would move on to the next pushcart. Once or twice, he would pick a toy of some kind and look at it, then at me; as if to suggest this might be something I might like. But I was ten years old and a good deal beyond just a toy.

"Only two or three more pushcarts remained. My father looked up, too, and I heard him jingle some coins in his pocket. In a flash, I knew it all. He'd gotten together about seventy-five cents to buy me a Christmas present. And he hadn't dared say so in case there was nothing to be had for so small a sum.

"As I looked up at him, I saw a look of despair and disappointment in his eyes that brought me closer to him than I had ever been in my life. I wanted to throw my arms around him and say: 'It doesn't matter ... I understand. This is better than a chemistry set or a printing press. I love you.'

"But instead, we stood shivering beside each other for a moment – then turned away from the last two pushcarts and started silently back home. I don't know <u>why</u> the words remained choked up within me. I didn't even take his hand on the way home – nor did he take mine. We were not on that basis. Nor did I ever tell him how close I felt that night. That, for a little while, the concrete wall between father and son had crumbled away. And I knew that we were two lonely people struggling to reach each other."

Two lonely people struggling to reach each other.

Who is that small December child struggling in loneliness to reach another? Well, you and are that December child.

Maybe – like Moss – it's been a hard year. Maybe, like him, we want terribly, not just a present this Christmas; but a token, a sign, that someone knows what we're going through and cares.

"And this shall be a sign unto you ..." sang the heavenly voices that first Noel in Luke 2:12. And what is that sign?

Nothing more than a small December infant, born homeless in a world where there is often little room for love. No decent housing, no clear paternity for this December child. Born in a barn, someplace in a backwater town, in the obscurity of the poor and defenseless.

André Malraux, France's first Minister of Cultural Affairs, believed that "beyond ourselves there is nothing or no one." He said that it is merely fate that has flung us like random atoms among the profusion of the earth and the galaxies of the stars.

No, says the audacious gospel. In our longing, in our common cry for eternal affirmation comes a sign; a small December child, whose name is Jesus.

He is the sign, the token that God – the center of all mystery – is not indifferent. But knows what we're going through and cares: deeply, tenderly, infinitely and comes to claim us and empower us with His love.

Out of the cosmic cold and eternal darkness comes this whisper down the wind in Luke 2:10. "… behold, I bring you good tidings of great joy, which shall be to all people."

You are loved, you are accepted, you are eternally important.

Princeton theologian Samuel Miller wrote, "This is the message of Christianity. The permanent structure of reality is not coercive, but persuasive." So God's sign to us is a small December babe, given into our keeping.

In one of his fine science fiction works, futurist Ray Bradbury describes a scene in Independence, Missouri, sometime in the not-too-distant future. The setting is much like that of 150 years ago; except that the pioneers, instead of heading West to settle, are preparing to go into outer space. The covered wagons have been replaced by space vehicles.

A young girl, with much trembling of heart and nerve, is making ready to go to another planet to marry her fiancé who is already there. But before she leaves, in order to reassure herself that she is doing the right thing, she calls him on the space telephone. His reply is completely blotted out by electrical interference except for one word – love.

And on the strength of having heard that one word from him, she leaps into the unknown state of life in space.

This is the word that we have from God. Throughout all of our wondering, throughout all our remorse and self-doubt; the one word – love – comes leaping though over the miles, over the centuries – from Bethlehem.

In Jesus, the small December babe, God speaks that He loves you deeply, infinitely.

May you – amidst all of the clamor of life – hear that word.

Prayer: Help me know that you know what I'm going through. And help me feel your love, in the gift of Jesus Christ.

Amen

THE SUMMERTIME OF THE SOUL

"Oh, those lazy, hazy, crazy days of summer," sang the late Nat King Cole – and we know exactly what he meant.

For July is the time for relaxation, for a change in pace, a pause in the rhythm of life. It is vacation time for so many. The word vacation, which comes from the old Latin word vacare "to be empty, to be free," means release from occupation, from the routine.

So, summer are the months when we are most apt to be free to do those things that we might not otherwise do in the busy year: read the book you've been meaning to get to, tackle the repair project you've been putting off, take the trip you've been wanting to make.

But there is, as Richard Nelson Bolles, a former Episcopal clergyman and author of the best-selling book, *What Color Is Your Parachute?* reminds us, a deeper significance to July than all of this.

July, he says, is something more, "something symbolic and mystical and deep. For somehow, half-forgotten within us, there is the instinctive feeling that the calendar is a kind of mirror to our lives. And in each month, we see another chapter unfold."

It's an intriguing suggestion, which Bolles makes. That, somehow, months correspond to, and indeed reflect, the various seasons of a person's life.

Apply that concept for a moment to your own life.

You begin with the first month, January – a month of beginnings, of birth, as it were. When you are first ushered into a world that indeed may seem cold and inhospitable or at least new.

Then, along come February and March – months that mirror your childhood, when you explore, play, discover, and fantasize as children often do in wintry wonderlands.

Then comes April – a month of budding and blossoming, just as in adolescence you begin to unfold toward the kind of person you want to be. Blossoming toward your own identity, as a person.

Then come May and June – months of springtime dances, months of brides and grooms, as you move out into full adulthood, fall in love, become expansive.

Then, July and August – golden months of your maturity, yet months filled with contradictory climates, with sudden and unpredictable moods in weather.

Then September – when, as German-born composer Kurt Weill wrote in *September Song*, "the days grow short when you reach September and dwindle down to a precious few …".

Beyond September lie the harvest months of October and November – when that which you sewed and planted in springtime and nurtured through the seasons is now gathered in. When hymns of thanksgiving can be sung for all the various experiences and the richness of life itself.

And at last, says Bolles, we come to our life's December. The time when our "thoughts are turned toward the heavens and stars, Messiah and new birth." And at the very end of December, he writes, comes New Year's Eve … a promise as the old dies so the new will come. Even as beyond the death of this life, lies the promise of new life for the faithful. Beginning again; wiser, stronger, with our hand placed firmly in God's.

If this poetic analogy of the calendar as a mirror of life cycle catches your imagination, you might ask: what about July? What does this particular time, this specific season of life mean?

In the sweep of my life's journey and pilgrimage, what does July offer me?

Well, for one thing, it offers a chance to pause, to change pace. To reflect upon and to evaluate the meaning of your life as a person -- your inner meaning. And it offers a chance to chart your direction in the future, based upon where you've been in the past.

This, of course, presupposes that you have matured somewhat. You've come through the stormy period of testing in adolescence. You've gained the many experiences of life for which you hungered as a young adult. It presupposes that, in the words of one psychiatrist, you have "become or are becoming, your own person."

It's a time to ask yourself: what am I to do with all of these experiences I've acquired – and am still acquiring? Such a question is very deep and searching. Each one of us will answer it differently.

But some may try to cut this probing question short with a fairly superficial response. Some may conclude that the best use we can find for our cumulative experiences -- for all that has gone before in shaping and defining us as persons -- is to puff ourselves up at the expense of others.

"In comparison with others," one might say, "see how fully I have lived; more deeply, more passionately, than any of my contemporaries. Everyone else who started where I did is so commonplace, by comparison. I've become much more worldly and wise, much more liberated and sophisticated. Because I – unlike them – have really lived!"

Or others may try to cut the questions short in the opposite way – by concluding that the best use we can find for our experiences is to put ourselves down.

A cartoon in the New Yorker shows a man in the July of his life musing aloud to his spouse: "It seems like only yesterday I was on the verge of getting it all together!"

The implication is that he never has – nor ever will.

"See what a failure I am. Others have found continuity, something solid upon which to structure and build their lives. But there is nothing I can point to and say, 'Here, I've really succeeded. Here, it all adds up.'"

But neither of these responses is the answer that you are meant to find in the July of your years.

Scripture offers us, time and again, clear directions in formulating our response to the question: What use am I intended to find for the experiences of my life? How can I understand where I've come from – and where I am to go?

Now, one of the most well-known and most cherished verses in scripture is found in Saint Paul's first letter to the Corinthian church in which he wrote that faith, hope and love abide – these three: but the greatest of these is love.

And those words cast light upon the question of what I am to do with my experiences in life.

Faith is a word which looks backward; over the past, when I was accumulating significant experiences. Faith is the perspective that helps me make sense of the formative years of my life. For it has to do with the foundation, the ground on which I stand.

Hope is the reaching out for something yet to come. The thrust to the future, the attitude toward the direction I choose yet to go.

Love is now; being and acting in the here and now.

It is the clue to what we are to do with all the experiences we have accumulated; when we come to the July of our lives.

People have always wanted to leave something lasting behind. But only the mighty or the highly gifted have the chance to do this through history or the arts. Everyone, however, leaves something; which outlasts the greatest fame or accomplishment. When she or he reaches out -- even for a few moments -- in loving another.

Love is what lasts. And this – says the Christian gospel – is what life is all about. God seeks and loves us through the many experiences of our lives. That we, in turn, may become instruments of His love.

You are to use your experiences, then, to reach out in love. Here is where you find purpose and point and meaning to your existence.

Have you, in the years before your July, ever had the experience of being lonely? Then use it, to reach out <u>now</u> to those who are lonely around you.

Have you had the experience of being a stranger in a group? Then use it <u>now</u> to reach out to those who are strangers in your group.

Have you had the experience of being afraid? Then use it <u>now</u> to reach out to those who are afraid around you.

What experiences have been yours? Being sick? Being healed? Being depressed? Being comforted? Being up? Being down?

Then, take these experiences -- and use them all to reach out with empathy. To those about you, who are <u>now</u> in the same condition, wherever you encounter them -- in your home, your place of work, wherever you are.

That is the answer to the question of the July of our lives.

Look back then, over the months of your life -- in faith. Remember gratefully all, which the Lord of life has given you -- in rich experience. And look forward to all the time yet to come -- in hope. In confidence and with trust that your life will be woven into the greater mosaic which the Lord of the years fashions.

But for <u>now</u> – for always – use your experiences to love and to affirm others; and to enter into their experiences with a strengthening touch.

This is the gift and the opportunity that your July offers you.

Prayer: Dear Lord, let me live with the faith that my experiences were part of your plan for me, with the hope that my future holds your promise, and live now with the purpose of loving others as you have loved me.

Amen

THE TIME OF OUR LIVES

There is something significant about the passage of time; memories flood in upon us, questions about the future open before us.

It is a time when time itself becomes qualitative, different for us. Ordinarily, we Americans deal with time as a commodity. One of our favorite mantras puts it this way: "time is money." And the former Ambassador to Japan, Edwin Reischauer, said that while the Japanese have perfected the use of space, we Americans have perfected the use of time -- to the nth degree.

So, culturally, we are a people who have almost religious feelings about time: it is something very important to us.

If you don't believe it, think how you feel when you get caught on a freeway during rush hour, or lined up at a restaurant that doesn't take reservations, or even trying to get through the check-out stand in the supermarket the day before Thanksgiving.

We are a time–conscious people; programmed to make the most of our time, to dispose of it efficiently and purposefully. And when we understand that, we are at once back in the world in which St. Paul and the early Christians lived.

For ancient Rome was also very time-conscious. The Romans, above all, were great organizers. They worried about schedules, sequences, and deadlines. They drove themselves and others ruthlessly.

They, too, lived as fast as they could. Why? Because they were having the time of their lives!

Ironically, when their mighty Empire reached its zenith, when it became world encompassing and prosperous; it was precisely then that a cloud of worry and anxiety descended. They feared that they might lose all that they had gained.

And as the oppressive weight of time – with its drift toward decay and insecurity grew, they began to drive themselves toward all forms of escapism.

An astute observer like Saint Paul could surely see the pattern in it. There was escaping the dread of time, by work. Roman businessmen drowned their fear by working all the harder. Or, they escaped the burden of time by the wildest kinds of self-indulgence: gluttony and circuses, orgies of pleasure and bestiality.

Or, they escaped the anxiety of time by attempting to overcome time through religious cults and rituals. At the time of Paul, Rome had more sects and cults than we have in the U.S. – which is saying a lot. Historically, almost any kind of religious practice can flourish here; from the most bland and benign to the most bizarre and malevolent.

It was that way in the Rome of the first century. Disillusioned with their own waning heritage, millions turned toward rituals, rites, and even secret words. All to purchase something, which might dispel the wasting rush of time.

Now, unlike their contemporaries, the early Christians dealt with time in a different manner. They were not anxious about the movement of time. They did not seek to escape the threat of death, which time brings with it.

Rather, they saw time as a gift. Time for the Christian was a beautiful gift and it was short. They believed that the end of man's organized use of time was just around the corner, when Christ would come in glory.

Yet, this belief did not lead to an escape from responsible and caring living. Just the opposite. For in Jesus Christ – in his life, death and resurrection – Christians knew that there had been a decisive, once-and-for-all breakthrough in human existence.

Life – thank God – would never be the same. Time would never be the same.

Christians added another word for time itself. No longer was it just chronos; something which could be measured, in terms of duration. Now time was kairos; capable of depth, of quality, of revealing the One whom Jesus called Father. Eternity intersected ordinary time.

And so Paul could write to his fellow Christians to live life with a sense of responsibility. Not as people who do not know the meaning and purpose of life, but as those who do. Use your time wisely.

Time counted because God was lovingly, redemptively involved in it.

Cynics can remind us that, of course, the early Christians were mistaken. Christ didn't return and consummate time when they thought He would.

The world plainly did not come to an end.

So, where is the apostle Paul? Where are the early Christians? Where, for that matter, are the frantic Romans?

Well, they are all dead. Time ran out for them.

They died – each of them on the day appointed for them. And on that day, the end of their individual world occurred. Each one of them experienced that judgment of cessation which death inevitably means.

Before we dismiss Paul and the early church and its ethic on the use of time, though, perhaps we had better take another look.

In 2 Peter 3:10, Jesus warned his disciples not to speculate about the circumstances or the timetable of His coming. "But the day of the Lord will come as a thief in the night."

And so it is; things always end sooner than we think.

The foolish Romans were right: doom did hang over them. Not only because their civilization was decaying from within, but also because they were finite and mortal. Just as we are finite and mortal, too.

So Paul was right. Make the most of time, he suggests, for time is short. He was right, even when he seemed wrong; there is no time to waste.

But what did he mean? He meant now is the time to respond to God's promptings. To turn around and open yourself to the One who seeks you. And thus, find a new focus, a new point, a new meaning in your existence.

By letting the kairos happen in you. So, that each day is received as a gift, a new day to draw close to God. Or rather, to let Him enter into your life and consciousness. And so change the way in which you relate to yourself and to others.

You cannot redeem your past – it is gone. But you need not try;

because God, through the gift and sacrifice of Jesus Christ, lays claim on your past and speaks forgiveness.

You cannot redeem your future – and it is ridiculous to confuse Christianity with some sort of celestial insurance policy. God cannot be bribed.

But you can redeem the present -- by letting the God who seeks you enter into your own history, your own mind and heart. And accepting the One who accepts you – as you are: past, present and future.

That's how time is redeemed. This kind of time is not money; it cannot be purchased. It is a gift. Given in love by the God who, in Jesus Christ, enters your time and my time with healing, with affection, with love.

May this time happen to you today!

Prayer: Dear God, let me accept the present of your presence in my life. It's about time!

Amen

TO LIVE IS TO CHOOSE

The 56-year-old managing editor of the Tulsa Oklahoma Tribune, Gordon Fallis published a remarkable narrative of his choice to die one night – and then, the reversal of that decision in a split-second choice to live.

He writes of driving out to a nearby dam, surveying the black, swirling waters. Just as he was about to plunge in, a car he hadn't seen approached, slowed down and then stopped. "Kind of dangerous on that side of the railing, isn't it?" the young driver asked.

Fallis mumbled something about fishing, and the young man drove off.

Listen to his words: "I was alone again. Never in my wildest dreams could I have imagined the events in my life that would put me on the edge. Personal, degrading circumstances that ruin people's lives and business experiences that continually weaken the fibers … leading to fear and frustration.

"The car had gone only to the end of the bridge and was turning around! I jumped. Hitting the water was like being swatted with a giant paddle. It stung. My head throbbed.

"From the depths, as always, I surfaced. The spot from which I had jumped was miles above me. My legs were paddling, but not because of my conscious thought. I was staying afloat."

How do you die in water? Lie face down? Let the current drag you out and under? Stop breathing? You can NOT just stop breathing. It's impossible. Instantly, he knew he was a live-er … not a die-er. It had taken him more that 50 years to live this life, but the review took only moments. He swam.

He tells of swimming back and forth, fighting the current, of the exhaustion. And the miracle of being found, rescued; the understanding of people, and the assurance from a physician who said: "You were suicidal, but you are not now."

And he concluded his account with these words: "If this recitation can bring just one person from the bottom of life back to the top or near the top; I will feel the public humiliation I am experiencing not to have been in vain."

In the Book of Deuteronomy 30:19, the Lord announces that he has set before Israel a choice between "life and death, blessing and curse: therefore, choose life …"

In a moment of self-clarification, in a revelatory moment, in the darkness of the water, while bent on death; Gordon Fallis chose life. Or, perhaps in some sense, we could say that life chose him.

It is, of course, the most profound choice that any of us can ever make. And it is also, in a very real sense, a choice, which we must make again and again. And that is so because living has much more to do than merely existing. Living has to do with <u>how</u> we exist and <u>for whom</u> we exist and <u>for what purpose.</u>

Living has to do with the quality of our attitude towards ourselves and others.

"Therefore, choose life …" says the Old Testament. The writer of Deuteronomy was attempting to call Israel from its ongoing fascination with and worship of idols. He portrayed such worship as the way leading to death and oblivion, a dead-end street.

Why? Idols are always projections of some dimension of our human experience – of power, or sexuality, or whatever. And to worship such projections is, ultimately, therefore to worship one's self.

And whenever the self turns in on itself, centers its existence on itself, it inevitably withers, loses something of itself, and ultimately dies. Only when life is centered outside the self, can you really find yourself. Only then, can you find breathing room and playfulness.

People, who center their lives on themselves, lose themselves. We were created for relationships with others, with the world and ultimately, with God. Not the god of our own making, our projections or our own wishes; but the One who summons us to covenant, to mission, and to the fuller life intended for us.

"For whosoever will save his life, shall lose it: and whosoever will lose his life, for my sake shall find it," said Jesus in Matthew 16:25-26. And then He asks: "For what is a man profited, if he shall gain the whole world and lose his own soul?"

Thus, we are all engaged in the recurring choice of life and death. Between the siren call to worship the narrower self and the larger call to worship that center of life outside ourselves -- even the mystery and majesty of God.

We are creatures who can make choices. And we define ourselves through our choices; a process by which we discover and actually become who we are.

In choice making, there is a scale of values, those things we find worthwhile.

Writes Swiss physician, Paul Tournier, "Underlying every decisive choice; there is thus a prior, fundamental choice. A spiritual one, the choice of one's God: What is your God?" he asks. "Your mother, your own self interest, your instincts, your pleasure, reason, science or Jesus Christ?"

To make a fundamental choice is, inevitably, to affirm one center of existence over against another; to choose one thing is, in some sense, not to choose another.

Choosing means renouncing. Robert Frost puts it eloquently:

> "Two roads diverged in a yellow wood,
> And sorry I could not travel both
> And be one traveler, long I stood
> And looked down one as far as I could
>
> "Two roads diverged in a wood, and I—
> I took the one less traveled by,
> And that has made all the difference."

Any of us can say the same -- whenever we tell one another our own personal stories. Our journeys as human beings – journeys, which involve choice, choice informed by faith. Without faith, there is never any organizing principle to life; no center for existence.

The question, then, is: Faith in what? In ourselves? In some projection of our human desires? Or in the One who summons us to make a basic choice. For the Christian, to say "Yes," to life means saying "No," to the narrower self.

Now, we should not pretend that this is ever a completed matter; it isn't. Nor are our choices ever 100% pure or perfect. We aren't and our choices aren't.

But the gospel of Jesus Christ brings good news for people who are imperfect, who are not consistent. It frees us from believing that we have to pump security and meaning into our own lives, by our own efforts and choices.

God's grace and His flexibility are such that even mistaken situations, muffed opportunities, messy choices can yet be redeemed.

So, we who are summoned to choose life do not have to be uptight about our lives. We don't have to take ourselves so seriously or soberly. Why? Our ultimate confidence comes not from our own power, but in that center which is outside ourselves: God's active, strong love for us in Jesus Christ.

I think that is what Martin Luther meant when he said, "Sin boldly!"

That is, recognize our human dilemma. Recognize that always our choices are made in self-centeredness, with some touch of insecurity and anxiety.

Yes. Recognize all of that. But recognize something much more: the fact that God is _for_ us. His love for us goes to the very depths of human experience. Nothing can nor will cancel out His commitment to us.

His love allows us to choose life, to grow, and to enter into human experiences more deeply and compassionately. And even in the depths, we discover, as Gordon Fallis did, that life is the best choice of all!

Prayer: Dear Lord, let me choose a life in Christ that is courageous, full of heart and blessed by God.

Amen

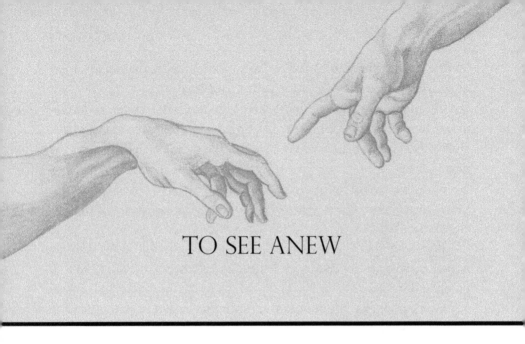

TO SEE ANEW

There is a story of the healing of a blind man in the Gospel of John. I caution you to remember that in John's Gospel, things are never quite as simple as they seem. Adhering to every event is layer upon layer of meaning.

So, it is with this story. It seems so straightforward. But John saw dramatic possibilities and chose to use them in order to instruct his readers; and strengthen in them their belief that Jesus is Messiah, the Light of the World.

It is a story, which starts with a blind man who will gain his sight. And ends with religious people who become increasingly blind, spiritually. I would encourage you to read the entire extended story, John 9:1-12 and ponder it.

But for now, let's examine the first part. The setting is plain: Walking along, Jesus and the disciples see great human need in the person of a blind beggar.

The disciples immediately ask a question: "Master, who did sin, this man or his parents, that he was born blind?"

The implication, here, is that people get what they deserve. If you suffer, you've obviously done something to deserve it. It's an idea as old as the book of Job; and as contemporary as many of the packaged salvation theories, which abound.

In a recent article, a mother wrote of her nine-year-old son. Jonathon died after six years of struggling with a disease diagnosed as Lupus, the Latin word for wolf. Prior to cortisone -- a drug that controls, but does not cure -- the face of the victim became so ravaged that it resembled that of a wolf.

She told of Jonathon's acceptance of the indignities he suffered in order to survive -- his patience, his boyish grace. She told, too, of the kindness and helpful gifts of others. But then she wrote:

"We live in a confusing age. For all of our medical miracles, there is no consensus as to the cause of the illness or the source of healing. We took Jonathon to healers, who measured his energy flow; and declared that something in him wanted to hang on to the disease. To psychotherapists, who concluded that the interpersonal relationships in the family were responsible. To nutritionists, who prescribed mega-vitamin therapy. To hypnotists and practitioners of visual imagery. Well-meaning acquaintances referred us to magazine articles that detailed spontaneous and miraculous remissions brought about by fasting, by vegetarianism, by medication. We meditated, we visualized, we fed Jonathon whole grains and fresh fruit; we eliminated sugar. We laughed a lot; we dealt honestly with his anger and with our own; we refused to allow him to use his illness to manipulate.

"The miracle did not happen in the real world of pills and therapies. Jonathon did not get better. Toward the end, when the disease had reached the central nervous system; I could finally bring myself to wish -- because I loved him very much -- that he would die."

Who sinned ... the parents? the boy? There are plenty of people today who really do subscribe to the monstrous cruelty that people simply get what they want. As if, for example, forms of life hostile to our own -- such as predatory viruses -- do not exist. Or, as if, a brutalized, burned, beaten child really chose her fate.

How comforting such a view is to those who do not suffer! For, it reassures us of our own virtue, our own wholeness. And absolves us from any sense of connection with those who are different, less whole than we.

Jesus was not one of us. He rejected such hypocritical and sanctimonious talk. Rather, He focused on the purpose -- not the cause -- of each one's blindness: " ... that the works of God should be made manifest in him."

The need must first be met with action. Reflection could come later.

In his miracle of restoring sight to the man, Jesus "spat on the ground and made clay of the spittle and He anointed the eyes of the blind man with the clay.

"And said unto him, Go, wash in the pool of Siloam ... he went his way therefore, and washed, and came seeing.

"The neighbours therefore, and they which before had seen him that he was blind, said, 'Is not this he that sat and begged?'

"Some said, 'This is he:' others said, 'He is like him:' but he said, 'I am he.'

"Therefore said they unto him, 'How were thine eyes opened?'

"He answered and said, A man that is called Jesus ...."

In his gospel, John's purpose is not to focus upon the miracle itself, but rather to understand it as a sign. A sign that points to who Jesus really is. By enabling this man to change his condition from darkness to light, from blindness to sight, Jesus reveals himself .

Try to imagine what happened to the blind man sent to wash in the healing waters; the swift shattering of the darkness of a lifetime, the opening of sightless eyes. What is this, but the characteristic work of Jesus still, for you and me and all the world? For the first time in his life, the man sees – what?

Four things. He sees the world around him – that first – the wonder and beauty of God's creation. He sees the faces of his fellow human beings, that next. He sees himself, his hands, his feet, perhaps his face in some mirror-like surface; showing him what kind of a man he is. And, finally, he sees Jesus, to whom he owes it all.

Aren't these precisely the four facts to which Christ opens our own eyes today:

He opens our eyes to the world. So, we can see something of the glory of God in the variety, the vastness, the mystery and otherness of creation.

He opens our eyes to our fellow beings. So, we may not think of them merely as so many faces on the street or cogs in a machine or numbers on a graph. But, everyone is now a child of God, for whom Christ lived and died.

He opens our eyes to ourselves. To the reality of our own uniqueness, our own ambiguous stance; as creatures caught in the flow of time. Yet, are able to transcend time through memory and imagination. Creatures, capable of grandeur and yet, vexed with misery. And always, in need of wholeness.

We can see our own terrible need for something beyond the madness in which whole nations, no less than you and I, are involved. Yet, we can see that the last word to be spoken about us is that we are infinitely precious and valuable. Inhabiting a life, which can be the arena for the deepest and most redeeming love.

And so, our eyes are open then to Jesus himself. So, that He is no longer someone we read about in a book or hear of in a church or argue about in a discussion group. But, He is the living presence in our lives. The one true light that allows us to illuminate and interpret everything else.

This is what happens when the Lord touches us and lets us see.

There is one other layer of meaning. For in the washing at the pool, John sees a sign for the sacrament of baptism. The scene of the blind man bathing at Siloam is found on numerous walls of the catacombs in Rome – as early Christians depicted baptism in art.

As one becomes a Christian and confesses Christ, one becomes "en-lightened."

Think for a moment of your own baptism. We live in a society preoccupied with surfaces. Where, unless we break out of self-concern, we simply cannot see beyond the surface. We remain, somehow, not just lonely (for at least a lonely person can see outside himself) but cut-off, alone, removed from the depths. And the heights.

By baptism, you are placed into community – a covenant community – that, through its rhythms, its seasons, its worship, reconnects you again and again to that which is eternal, larger.

Swedish translator, Brita Stendahl of Cambridge, in her book, *Sabbatical Reflections*, speaks of the function of Sunday worship:

"It gives us back the week for judgment and forgiveness. The purpose of worship is not to hear a sermon, to sing a hymn or two. It is something much larger; to come in contact with the world as it is and as we want it to be; both, at the same time.

"That's why it looks so silly to an outsider and observer who objects to the seemingly easy transition, not knowing that it is not easy at all. It is an ongoing process. Sunday after Sunday after Sunday. It is not a habit; it is discipline and discipleship.

187

"In one short hour to moan and to mourn and then to forget oneself and join with joy, the others. In mock banquet, reminding us of bread: hunger, wine: blood, life: death, and resurrection. The hope that defies despair. You don't do that in an hour – the hour becomes only a manifestation of what it takes a lifetime to realize.

"The hour spent in church is irreplaceable. When I now leave for church on Sunday morning and return an hour and a half later, I can hardly believe such a short time has elapsed. What could I have done in that length of time? Read a little, think somewhat, listen to music, finish a review, prepare a meal, yes. But compared to the cosmic importance and personal engagement that has taken place in church – <u>no</u>, it cannot be compared. Church time is eternal."

It is the privilege of touching Heaven every week for an entire hour. From darkness of surface society into the community that is filled with the light of Jesus Christ; a real world of real issues and real people. We are called to receive, to give. Come to table – His table – receive a new sight, and go – to shed light.

Prayer: Lord, help me see and share the Light of your love

Amen

UNCERTAINTY & FAITH

In one of her earlier works, *Slouching Towards Bethlehem*, the brilliant novelist, Joan Didion, tells of the anxiety that stirred in her upon hearing that a popular hero of her childhood was seriously ill.

It seemed, somehow, to call everything into question.

"In John Wayne's world," she wrote, "John Wayne was supposed to give the orders. 'Let's ride,' he would say and saddle up. Forward ho – a man's got to do what he's got to do.

"'Hello there,' he said, when he first saw the girl in a construction camp or on a train or just standing on the front porch waiting for somebody to ride up through the tall grass.

"When John Wayne spoke, there was no mistaking his intentions; he had a sexual authority so strong that even a child could perceive it. And in a world we understood early to be characterized by corruption, doubt and paralyzing ambiguities; he suggested another world. One, which may or may not have ever existed, but in any case, exists no more.

"A place where a man could move freely, could make his own code and live by it. A world in which, if a man did what he had to do; he could one day take the girl, go riding through the draw and find himself home free. Not in a hospital with something going wrong inside; not in a high bed with flowers and the drugs and the forced smiles. But there, at the bend in the bright river, the cottonwood shimmering in the early morning sun."

189

Now, all of us can identify with this kind of longing and wistfulness for a more certain, a more simple and stable kind of world, which Joan Didion so vividly portrays.

We all know that we live in a time when problems are enormously complex, when simple solutions no longer seem possible. Perhaps, that is why we continue to portray the past as "the good old days." Which, on close examination, never prove to be that good at all. Perhaps, that hunger for simplicity and security is what fuels our preoccupation with nostalgia … seeing the past without its pain.

Life in our era is complex and ambiguous. And so great are problems that we might be characterized, all of us, as sufferers of complexity shock; nothing is simple, secure, or black and white, anymore.

And so, we are vulnerable to all sorts of movements, which beguilingly offer us what we lack.

Two examples come to mine. Some years ago, *Psychology Today* carried an article by Harvey Cox, sympathetically tracing the reasons why a number of young Americans have become consumers of certain Oriental religions. One of the reasons is a quest for authority. People have turned East to find truth, to lay hold of a message or a teaching in which they can believe and trust.

They join various groups, Cox maintains, as refugees from uncertainty. Often stressing the role of a particular guru whose wisdom or charismatic power has caused such a change in their lives.

Writes Cox: "Large numbers of people have begun to suffer a choice-fatigue. They hunger for an authority that will simplify, straighten out, assure; something or somebody who will make their choices fewer and less arduous."

That's one example. Another can be found in a *TIME* cover story entitled, "Why we behave as we do." It reports the emergence of a controversial theory of human behavior called sociobiology – a discipline, which tries to combine sociology and biology. And purports to find the answers for all human behavior, comprehensively, in the impersonal drive of genes to survive.

Do you see what's happening? In an age of great complexity and uncertainty, two movements have become very popular. On the one hand: People embrace a kind of transcendental, mystical simplicity and certainty.

On the other hand: People embrace a theory, which finds life reduced to the inherent, the horizontal, the natural; in which complexity is reduced to a minimum.

Now, the intensity of the search for certainty in an uncertain age is understandable. Without something to believe in or around which to organize experience – life loses its focus and thrust, its continuity and meaning.

Rev. Dr. Deryl Fleming writes:

"It's as though one's life is a store into which some mysterious presence creeps each evening after closing hours, and changes all the price tags around. The value of any and everything changes from day to day, according to the Dow Jones average or the latest fads and fashions.

"Having never developed a faith strong enough to carry them in a world of complexity, ambiguity and contradictions; some try hard and unsuccessfully to ignore such realities.

"It cuts the nerve of living meaningfully in this world and turns to a belief in nothing, lacking all conviction. So committed are they to being open-minded, they never get close enough to make a commitment.

"Unwilling to commit themselves until all the evidence is in, they ignore the fact that all the evidence will never be in – and that life is built on commitments. Afraid to risk themselves beyond being 'reasonable,' they overlook the reality that at its farthest and keenest edge, life is spirit rather than flesh. Soul rather than body, intangible rather than tangible, faith rather than reason."

I think Dr. Fleming is quite right: we are so constructed as human beings that we cannot live in a vacuum. We must make choices. And to do so always involves risk and a leap of faith.

The question then becomes a matter of the adequacy of faith. Of finding a faith around which we can live and yet which will allow us room for growth, for revision, for changing one's mind. Years ago, Harry Emerson Fosdick (whom Martin Luther King Jr. regarded as "the greatest preacher of this century") preached a sermon on "The Importance of Doubting Our Doubts." In it, he articulated a critical insight into doubt and faith. Only when you doubt your doubts are you truly free.

Biblical religion leaves room for that, my friends. It is candid. "For now we see through a glass, darkly," wrote the Apostle Paul in 1 Corinthians 13:12. "But then shall I know even as also I am known."

Biblical religion does not eliminate the mystery, which is built into life, into our own personal existence. Nor does it offer simple and easy solutions to the problems that vex us. Nor does it assure us the kind of certainty, which eliminates the need for faith.

"We walk by faith ... not by sight" (2 Corinthians 5:7) is the promise of Biblical religion.

And in that Biblical tradition, just as important as the answers it does offer are the questions it also raises. Faith is involved in hearing those questions; in learning how to phrase them anew, in our own language, from our own experience, in our own prayers.

There are, thank God, some things in life where certainty is possible, where certainty is necessary. But in most areas of life, we live by faith – because absolute certainty just isn't possible.

Theologian Paul Tillich wrote: "Faith includes an element of immediate awareness, which gives certainty <u>and</u> an element of uncertainty.

To accept this is courage ..."

Well, we really don't want to be that courageous, do we? We want more. We want certainty. But did you ever think, for instance, that Jesus wanted it too? When he prayed that the cup of suffering might be taken from Him; when he cried out in anguish in Psalm 22:1, "My God, my God, why hast Thou forsaken me? Why art Thou so far from helping me ...?" No certainty.

But, he didn't stop there. In Luke 23:46, Jesus affirmed: "Father, into thy hands, I commend my spirit." And his human life was taken, but his eternal life assured. That's what we get through the Bible. In Romans 8:28, we read: "And we know that all things work together for good to them that love God." And that is enough.

You know, in the most significant dimensions of life, we all must venture out in faith, without certainty. We become involved intimately with someone – we care about that other one – we invest ourselves – we link our destiny with the other one. That's an act of faith, no guarantees; no certainty.

We accept a new job – or we move to a new community – those are acts of faith, not certainty. Even believing in God is an act of faith – it isn't blind, but it is still faith.

And it neither eliminates the hard questions nor provides easy answers.

But it does mean, my friends, that we are open then, to a power beyond our own limited powers. We are not left alone in our strivings, our uncertainties, and our risk-taking. We have the presence in our lives of a compassionate Companion as we grope and grow and faith our way through life.

We may not be certain about everything, including some of our own religious beliefs. But, in faith, we are linked to One who is certain, who is <u>for</u> us and <u>with</u> us.

Prayer: Dear Lord, let me commit my life to Thee through faith.

Amen

WHEN THE JOURNEY IS TOO GREAT

"One small step for man, one giant leap for mankind." It was the summer of 1969, and the Apollo 11 crew walked on the moon for the first time in history.

But among the difficulties the 3-man crew and family bread-winners experienced on earth before leaving was the impossibility of affording life insurance for themselves as astronauts. So, Neil Armstrong, Buzz Aldrin and Michael Collins created a plan of their own to support their families; if something bad happened on their journey. Before the mission, when all three astronauts were in pre-launch quarantine, they signed hundred of autographs each and sent them to a friend. The plan was that if they didn't return from their mission, the entrusted friend was to send the autographed memorabilia to each of the astronaut's families. This way, they could make some money by selling the signatures of the Apollo 11 crew.

Another little-known fact was that shortly before Buzz Aldrin disembarked the spacecraft to join Neil Armstrong for that first historic moonwalk; he paused and un-stowed packages of bread and wine. Then, he placed them on a table in front of the abort guidance system computer, to remember Christ in a symbolic way.

That action thrilled millions of Christians and religious folk on earth. It was a dramatic act, which pointed beyond itself to the mystery that encompasses life in its heights and depths.

Buzz Aldrin was a hero of faith and action. But after his safe return, earthbound once more, he began to suffer a profound depression. Success had perhaps been achieved at the price of robbing him of any further imaginable goal in life. He had done what he wanted to do. What else was left?

He had fulfilled his mission – the expectations others had for him and which he had for himself. Now what? Gradually, Aldrin found himself sinking into an ennui, a listlessness; preoccupied, blocked from any creative stirrings, becoming reclusive, his marriage strained. And all the while, afraid to admit that this was happening to him, fearful of letting others see what was going on – a kind of unraveling at the very peak of success.

It is said that the great generals of history were never as dangerous as the day after defeat. So, some of us are never as vulnerable as the day after victory. The hero and heroine discover that there are no permanent or lasting victories. And without the thrill of victory, he or she is out of character, afraid, despairing.

We expect our astronauts or other role models and leaders to be always strong, cool, confident and unflappable. They must not admit to others – or themselves – those fears and anxieties, which plague the weak and passive.

In his book *Tough Hope, Sermons to Steer Around the Potholes in the Road of Life* author Clifford Schutjer reports on a study of suicide and physicians. And the fact that more than a fourth (28%) of all physicians who die before the age of 40 do so by taking their own lives. And moreover, those physicians specializing in psychiatry lead the group.

Perhaps, even more startling is the fact that the typical young physician who commits suicide is tops as a professional, has been trained at one of the most prestigious medical schools, and typically graduated highest in the class. In short, a promising leader, excelling in brilliance and competence.

The report concludes that one of the things to beware of is the false notion that somehow, a physician's knowledge and training immunizes him or her against emotional conflicts. That notion seems to lead to an unwitting neglect by friends, family and colleagues; who rationalize complacency, reassuring themselves that "after all, as physicians, they know how to take care of themselves."

The expectations for super-human behavior abound. Familial relationships are laden with assumptions:

> "Good old dad/mom – he/she will understand; he/she can take it, don't worry about him/her.

> Or a friend or neighbor – so stable, so full of energy.

> Or an executive, or sometimes even ourselves: "I'm too strong to grieve," "I'm too tough to fall apart," "I'm too competent ever to be out of control."

In the spiritual realm, this gets translated into a moralistic Christianity. If you are <u>really</u> a Christian, you will be courageous and never afraid. Pure in thought and never stirred by lust. If you are a <u>real</u> Christian, you'll be happy and not troubled by depression. Always loving and understanding, you'll be able to avoid anger or apathy. If you have genuine faith, you'll never be troubled or tormented by doubt or unbelief.

How very cruel, how very dehumanizing, all of this is. We may have been conditioned, hopefully, to feel empathy for those who are emotionally disabled in some obvious way. But the flip side is that we imprison others and ourselves, with images of invulnerability, demanding strength in all areas of life.

When moralism prevails, the good news of the gospel gets perverted into bad news. Instead of liberating us with the news that we are held in the constraint of a greater love, which accepts us as we are, which seeks to elicit our growth; we get imprisoned into expectations, which force us to deny who we are and where we really live.

We keep forgetting that time and again, Jesus revealed himself as needy, as vulnerable. Someone, who needed some reassurance. Whose life depended upon the strength and nourishment of the intimate band of people who he had sought and called.

You find that vulnerability in the Gospel. In the very chapter and verse of John 6:35 where Jesus makes this great "I am" statement: "I am the bread of life: he that cometh to me shall never hunger ...."

If you read on in John 6:66-67, you find that the very one who is to feed others, is himself hungry -- vulnerable."From that time many of his disciples went back, and walked no more with Him. Then Jesus said unto the twelve "Will ye also go away?"

The plaintiveness, the vulnerability in these words – resonates again in the scene in Gethsemane where Jesus almost begs them to just stay there – be with Him – pray with Him!

But, of course, He has to ask. Because who would think that secure, strong Jesus, the Son of God, would ever need the support, the understanding of others? Who isn't vulnerable at some level, at some time? Who doesn't experience the journey as too great? Every one of us.

The strong, too, have their limits; their moments when life comes crashing in upon them. All of us are both strong and weak; paradoxical creatures capable of giving much, but sometimes needing much. None of us are built simply to go it alone: we need resources, which meet our real needs.

Elijah (the strong man who collapses into despair at the moment of his success) finds this anew as he is bidden to rise and eat and receives the nourishment to let him continue his journey.

He needs -- and receives – the strength, which comes from without, in order to get himself into motion again. In order to replenish the strength he does have in himself, to summon his resources.

For our hunger, there is food. Food for the journey.

Where do we find it? From others – who, accepting us, help us accept ourselves. And behind this course – the greatest source of accepting – the love of God.

Prayer: Dear Lord, let me be the wind beneath the wings of others, holding them up when they stagger and fall, with love and understanding;

Amen

WHEN THERE'S NOTHING
YOU CAN DO

We Americans are known throughout the world for our activity, our ability to define problems and organize solutions for them. We are active people who <u>do</u> things!

As the once wry observer of Los Angeles' cultural scene, Art Seidenbaum wrote in the *Los Angeles Times*, we're even able to make a profit out of hard times. He noted classified ads that were promoting bankruptcy at the bargain rate of $49.95 – End debt/act now.

"There's no problem which can't be solved and can't be profitable," he wrote, with tongue-in-cheek. "Lonely? We can sell you a company. Uneducated? We can sell you a degree to hang on your wall without any additional homework."

Now behind the salty humor stands this truth: We are doers, movers, and solvers. And we all know the sense of inner-satisfaction, which comes from having faced some obstacle and overcoming it.

This exhilaration in actively "taking-charge" is a mark of our strength, confidence and optimism as a people.

But how do we respond when we confront those inevitable situations in life; when apparently, we are powerless to do anything effective at all? When we've exhausted all the alternatives, when nothing can be done?

These times come to everyone of us. No one is immune.

There are times when we confront something beyond our power to solve. When suddenly, we feel like powerless children lost in a deep woods; hoping to hear a voice, or to find a path or a guide to lead us out into the sunlight again.

We are thrown back, at such times, upon whatever spiritual resources we possess; we grope in the dark.

These times come to us in the ordinary rhythm of life. It can happen to parents, for example, who do everything they possibly can for their children. Then, the time comes, when the parents must let go; must allow the children to make their own decisions, choose their own direction, adopt their own goals and values.

And that can be very hard, very painful. For there is nothing you can do – but let them go. Even though you may know, that they are vulnerable to some very hurtful things out there in the world. With which they are not necessarily wise or experienced or prepared enough to cope.

But there is nothing to be done. For you can't live for them, you can't decide for them, you can't weep for them.

Spanish-born essayist, George Santayana, wrote to a bereaved mother who had lost her little boy:

"We have no claim to any of our possessions. We have no claim to exist; and as we have to die in the end, so we must resign ourselves to die piecemeal -- which really happens when we lose somebody or something that was closely intertwined with our existence. This would seem a wise attitude to take toward children. They are not possessions, we have no claim on them; they owe us nothing. They are lent to us, you might say, and are taken away by death, or, more commonly, by the natural process of growing up."

Philosopher Kahlil Gibran wrote similarly in *The Prophet*:

"Your children are not your children.
They are the sons and daughters of Life's longing for itself.
"They come through you but not from you,
And though they are with you yet they belong not to you.
"You may give them your love, but not your thoughts
For they have their own thoughts...."

It's hard – when you care – to confront a situation where you can do nothing more than what you have already done for your own flesh and blood.

We confront this, sometimes, with our friends, too.

Perhaps you have as friends – a married couple, for example – who begin to grow apart. They no longer relate positively to one another. They either withdraw from each other or break into open warfare and hostility similar to Martha and George in *"Who's Afraid of Virginia Wolfe."*

Maybe you care deeply about these friends. Maybe you want desperately to help. But you sense that there is no way in which you can help them resolve their tragic breaking apart.

You are a friend. And, therefore -- precisely because you care -- shun choosing sides, or give frail and possibly faulty advice, or intrude inappropriately.

Maybe that's one of those situations when you can do nothing. Maybe you can only <u>be</u> available – rather than <u>do</u> something: Being rather than doing.

That may be a way of responding to those times when we can do nothing. But, it's not an easy lesson to learn.

Have you ever experienced a situation where you felt utterly powerless?

A hospital corridor, for instance, where you waited and waited for some word from the surgeon. Where you are separated from your loved one. Where – you wish – in some way that you could bear at least part of that loved one's suffering, absorb part of the pain. But there is nothing you can do.

It is all out of your hands. You cannot act.

You can only wait – <u>be</u>ing there, living with your nagging fear, blunting in your mind the forces of decisions you hope not to have to make.

It is a lonely time – and it comes, in one form or another, to us all. A time

When we have to confront our own limitations,
When who we <u>are</u> counts for more than what we <u>do,</u>
When the soul stands exposed,
When there are no distractions, and the truth about us emerges.

Perhaps then, at those times, when we can do nothing; we learn to pray again. Not only asking for something: for strength, for courage, for affirmation beyond ourselves. But opening ourselves to our own depths, allowing the searchlight of truth to fall upon the hidden places of our inner-lives.

To discover, again, perhaps the sincerity which we might have forgotten in all our doing and acting.

Then, perhaps, we discover two things: that while we can do nothing for others whom we love and want to help; we can at least be present with them. As we are; that is all they need from us. Not actions, which we cannot take or even words, which we might not be able to speak. But simply to be with them as we are ...

> Trying not to give into the tug and pull we have toward self pity,

> Trying to face the long hours with as much cheer as we can muster,

> Trying to <u>be</u> ourselves.

And with that discovery comes another: that we are not alone in our powerlessness. That there is One who knows our need and who can replenish and renew our fragile resources. Helping us <u>be</u> for another, even when we cannot <u>do</u> much.

"O God, give us serenity to accept that which cannot be changed ..."

The same year that American theologian, Reinhold Niebuhr wrote that prayer, Eugene O'Neill wrote a play called *Days Without End*.

In it, the main character is like the man of the 21st Century -- torn between his aspiring self and his cynical self. Thinking he has outgrown God, yet seeking some sense to it all; who cries out that he is "sick of my life ...sick of myself."

But another character – a stumbling, bungling lost soul who has tried everything – at last comes upon an old church with a cross.

Like us all, he had seen dozens of crosses many times before.

But this time, it is different. This time, he sees the cross as a symbol of the Almighty Spirit of God, reaching down to a groping man, who is grasping at anything.

This time, he sees the cross as God's way of letting us know how ready He is to go through what we go through, to identify with us in our troubles.

So, the man stops trying to tell God how things must be. He begins to understand something about religious faith that many of us in our activism scarcely grasp. Real, transforming faith that carries us through a crisis does not depend so much on what we do, as on what we let God do.

Real faith does not come in our achieving (how we try to let God know how competent we are) but in our receiving.

And it is when we can sometimes do nothing – nothing at all – that we are open to receive. To receive power to be, power to examine ourselves and to be present in love with someone else.

On such occasions, it may seem that we are doing nothing at all. But we are really doing the most important thing of all: being.

Prayer: "O God, give me the serenity to accept that which cannot be changed. And let me not try to achieve but simply, to receive ... your love."

Amen

WHO AM I?

"We human beings," observed the rather austere philosopher who resided in the Black Forest of 20th Century Germany, Martin Heidegger, "have a facility for retreating from the mysterious to the manageable."

We may not be able to handle death, but we can busy ourselves with funeral details.

We cannot capture God, but we can lose ourselves in religious niceties.

We cannot fathom love, but we can occupy ourselves with the techniques of sex (so the complete sexual manual, *The Joy of Sex*, is followed by a sequel entitled – guess what – *More Joy!*)

Rarely do people, then, confront the aching question of meaning in life – although the question poses itself constantly. But there was a man – who scholars tell us lived a few centuries before the birth of Christ – who did confront the central question: Is existence meaningful?

We really know little about him. He is simply known as Koheleth – the preacher. And he wrote a little book found in the Old Testament – which is the most despairing of all the books in the Bible. It is the Book of Ecclesiastes.

If you are familiar with it in any way – your knowledge may be derived from words familiar in the pop tune written by Pete Seger: *Turn Turn Turn*

> To everything (turn, turn, turn)
> There is a season (turn, turn, turn)
> And a time to every purpose, under Heaven
>
> A time to be born, a time to die
> A time to plant, a time to reap
> A time to kill, a time to heal
> A time to laugh, a time to weep
>
> ….

But Koheleth's real message is that "under the sun" which is kind of code meaning "without God," everything is vanity.

"Vanity of vanities!" he cries in agony in Ecclesiastes 1:2, "All is vanity."

To prove that he wasn't fooling, Koheleth uses these words "all is vanity" some twenty-five times in his short chapter. Nothing counts for anything. Everything is vanity – and vanity, as a word, means emptiness, nothingness.

All human achievements – no matter whether you are the wisest Ph.D., the most handsome and winning of people, Man of the year – all are vanity.

And nothing in life is trustworthy, believes Koheleth: even nature – which appears to be so enduring, even the earth itself, is full of weariness. "The thing that hath been, it is that which shall be; and that which is done is that which shall be done: and there is no new thing under the sun," he writes in Ecclesiastes 1:9.

The Book of Ecclesiastes presents a challenge to casual Bible readers and academics alike. The book's theme and tone seem so contrary to the rest of Scripture. In fact, it's one of the few books of the Old Testament that the early Church debated not including in the Bible. But Koheleth has this great plus. He faces it directly; he stares into the center of things and finds – nothing.

Now and then, a few people rise up to confront the strong sense of the irrational, which does run through life.

In the 20th Century, Albert Camus echoes: yes – life is fundamentally absurd. All is vanity under an indifferent cosmos. And, as if to punctuate his thoughts, Camus died absurdly at 46 (just two years after winning the

Pulitzer Prize for Literature) in an automobile crash, with the ticket for his intended train trip in his pocket.

Well, at least one can respect the seriousness and the honesty of Koheleth and Camus. Not so the man who came to Jesus one fine day demanding that Jesus settle some dispute, some family squabble about inheritance and property.

Jesus retorts in Luke 12:15 "Take heed and beware of all covetousness. For a man's life consisteth not in the abundance of things which he possesseth."

Then, he offers a parable in Luke 12:20-21 – so precise that it needs no explanation – of a rich man hedonistically enjoying life – eating, drinking, making merry – whose soul is suddenly demanded: "Thou fool," said God, "this night thy soul shall be required of thee: then whose shall those things be, which thou hast provided?"

Even the money you may amass – well, you can't take it with you and someone else who did not toil will receive it. So far, Koheleth would nod in agreement: vanity.

But then, Jesus goes beyond that and drives home his point: "So, is he that layeth up treasure for himself and is not rich toward God."

Here, Jesus breaks company with Koheleth – and with all who despair of finding meaning in life. There is something higher in life to which a person can aspire; there is something of permanence beyond all which eventually disintegrates and disappears.

There is such a thing as richness toward God – a quality that relates you to that which is essential, which endures. Now, it may seem commonplace to say that there are two levels to existence – the temporal and the eternal. But, the point Jesus makes is startling: the eternal and the temporal are interfused, joined together.

The eternal isn't something out there, beyond us, indifferent to us while "down" below we work with our mortality tables, crime statistics and sin. No. Eternity intersects time.

This is how time gains its meaning and its abiding significance. However momentary our lives, they can be intersected by the eternal.

Ernest Campbell, a minister at New York City's Neo-Gothic Riverside Church in Morningside Heights, founded by John D. Rockefeller in 1930, and noted for its history of social justice, said: "We may be small, we may be brief, but we are a God-loved people in a God-loved world."

And to know this is to be rich toward God – and ultimately secure.

It is our insecurity that prompts us to try to find meaning in that which does not endure – or to despair of ever finding meaning at all. Strange creatures, we: finite, we hunger for that which transcends; temporal, we long for that which is permanent.

The covetousness – which Jesus spoke against – is simply a symptom of our insecurity – a desperate lack of ultimate confidence, the fear of letting go.

In the brilliant film, *The Apprenticeship of Duddy Kravitz,* we encounter a young man on the make, who puts in his apprenticeship and who learns his craft well. Layer by layer, the reasons for Duddy's insecurity and striving are exposed in the film: his older brother is the favored one, sent to medical school, manipulated for family pride. Duddy – with fierce determination to conquer: materialistically, sexually, finally does make it on his own – from street corner bar to land developer.

But along the way, he rejects trust, love, friendship – and in his moment of victory, at the apotheosis of his young career, we see the awful abyss open up – a soul filled with vanity, emptiness.

Our attempt to win permanence by ourselves is fruitless. We cannot ultimately save ourselves – and in this Koheleth is right. The attempts will always lead to vanity – for if nothing else mocks us, death will.

But it is precisely here -- here as we face the precarious quality of our existence – that good news, gospel comes: we are loved <u>as we are</u>. In our yearning, in our false starts and wrong directions to find permanence, we are claimed by a Love which itself bears our suffering.

In the life and death of Jesus Christ, God embraces and takes into himself the sting and hurts which are inflicted by the insecure. In the resurrection of Christ – a new destiny is opened for all people; a chance for new beginnings, in the light of a certain hope. Something new, eternally new, under the sun!

This new reality beckons to you in your search for meaning: to experience it is to discover the paradox. Mathematically, it may be true that the more you get, the more you have; but in human truth, the more you give away in love, the more you are and the more you become.

Resurrection truth is only known in faith -- which means in risk. Does life have hope – or is all in vain? That's a heavy question and deserves a serious answer. Felix Powell, the man who wrote the WWI marching song, *Pack Up Your Troubles in Your Old Kit Bag and Smile, Smile, Smile,* died a suicide. So did the man who wrote, *This is My Father's World*, Maltbie D. Babcock, after a bout with Mediterranean fever causing severe pain and depression.

The syndicated columnist and author, Jim Bishop spoke of the struggle for faith ….

"At the age of four, I knew that God was everywhere. I spoke to Him and sometimes He listened with sympathy. It was an unforgettable occasion in boyhood when He did indeed send a bicycle with a coaster brake! As I grew toward manhood, the more I learned, the less I believed in God. I told myself that He had been invented by ancients who feared the eternal darkness of death. Even worse, they had fashioned Him in their likeness.

"When I was 21, my superior intellect told me that God was a fake. Heaven could not be up and hell down; because in space, there is no up or down. And I knew that everything in creation dies, including the smallest insect and the biggest star."

But eventually, he began to doubt his doubts.

"Gradually, I lost faith in my intellect. It was far from supplying the needed answers. I could not see air, but without it I would die. Thus it is, I decided, with the spirit of man. I need something to breath life into a soul that has been crushed by the dominance of the human mind.

"Sometimes, lost in a labyrinth of complexities, I was forced to return to the beginning. Over and over, I argued with myself: (1) There is no God. (2) There is. Day by day, I began to see that nothing is accidental. All the "good" and "bad" events are part of a divine scheme in balance.

"I was a slow learner. But somehow, somewhere as I groped my painful way; I found my soul. Overnight, I knew it was there: wounded, bleeding perhaps, but alive!

"Faith does not come as quickly as these words. It starts. It stops. It floods and recedes. For a time, I felt that I was wooing faith. Cultivating it as one might a friend whom no one ever met. Grasping. Clawing. Reaching. Then calmness came. When I gave up, I could feel His presence.

There were no apparitions, no wraiths on the wall. He was there and I knew it."

Even though the faithful see life's meaning clearly – in the power of God's love which raises Christ from the dead – there are times when they may not see it so at all.

But they continue to act on the basis of the love they know and experience in Jesus Christ -- bearing witness on good days and bad days. Rich in the knowledge that life has an ultimacy and meaning beyond our brilliant denials or our frantic attempts to manufacture our own security.

Prayer: Heavenly Father, let me feel safe and secure in your Love.

Amen

WHO IS RIGHTEOUS?

The familiar words of Jesus from the Sermon on the Mount in Matthew 5:20: "For I say unto you, That except your righteousness shall exceed the righteousness of the scribes and Pharisees, ye shall in no case enter into the kingdom of Heaven."

Does that statement strike you as somehow incredible?

How, for instance, would you be more sober than sober? How could you be more righteous than scribes – jurists, interpreters of the sacred law? People of honor who kept the law in all of its demands? Or more than Pharisees – who were puritans, patriotic, generous to the poor, serious about upholding the highest form of obedience to the moral code?

And then why should Jesus say to them in Matthew 21:31: " ...the publicans (tax collectors) and the harlots go into the kingdom of God before you." What could this mean to any of us today?

Perhaps, as the MBA's do, we should begin with a case study – the history of a righteous man or woman.

A biography begins with this resolve: "I will present a good character or reputation before God and people." Nothing wrong with that, is there?

The legendary UCLA basketball coach, John Wooden was fond of saying: "Your reputation is who people think you are, your character is who you really are."

And after all, Benjamin Franklin kept a ledger of pros and cons in character and each night, added up what vices he had avoided. F. Scott Fitzgerald's famous character, Jay Gatsby kept a list, also: To improve himself and become socially acceptable.

But that may be the trouble: For life can't be simply lived by a code. Events intrude. Things change. Surprises – for good or worse – happen. Codes aren't that flexible. And in itself, a code can give no power for keeping a code; and no words to speak when a person violates it. Live by a rigid code and you tend to become rigid yourself.

Next step, in this case history. The "righteous" person says: "Well, at least, I'm not like that bad person over there."

Now, let's be clear about this: Some people, as psychiatrist M. Scott Peck reminds us in his book, *People of the Lie,* are bad. They are not to be emulated or admired. Pharisees spoke common sense: bad is to be avoided.

But the Pharisees were commonly held to have pretensions to superior sanctity, to be self-righteous persons -- hypocrites.

Pharisee means separated – separated in holiness. And, strangely, isn't that part of the problem. Should a person be so removed from others that s/he fails to see also his or her own solidarity as a human being sharing a common humanity?

Should we not acknowledge, at some level; that the very tendencies, the very impulses that lead to bad acts by others, also lie within us? That often, in the tissue-thin chambers of our hearts, the better angels of our nature dwell. Not far from the wolves, which howl in the basement of our souls?

Should we be so "separated' from our fellow human beings – from a recognition of a common humanity – that we avoid any thought, any awareness of others? A doctor, no matter how well trained and skillful, really isn't of much use, unless he or she is willing to treat disease and sickness, even at the risk of contagion.

Next step. The righteous person becomes uncomfortably aware that all goodness is entangled with badness. He or she must be separated in order to be a "good" person. But it is wrong to be separated from the world's needs.

Always, always there is the inevitable entanglement of good and bad. Life isn't simple. It is complex, deep, mysterious, intertwined. There are ambiguities to face.

There are often consequences, which we couldn't foresee and didn't intend. For instance, how many political revolutions in this century, and the last, have been launched in the name of liberty, only to end in a worse form of tyranny? And how many wars have been fought and continue to hold the world hostage in the name of religion?

The American essayist, Henry David Thoreau once remarked that if you see someone approaching with the intent to do you good, you should run for your life!

But the "righteous" can't acknowledge this ambiguity. Perhaps, at some deep level, they might be aware of it. But to admit it would involve breaking the rigid code by which they try to construct meaning. By which they try to validate their slippery existence (the right to be here), their justification for living.

And yet, to avoid the ambiguous and the complex is to avoid the pain that is necessarily involved in growth. I once heard a wise psychologist who works with three and four-year-old children describe how they enlarge their perceptions.

Like all of us, children try to make sense out of their experiences. They construct a world, if you will, where they understand relationships and find a place for themselves. But when their tiny world-view becomes too narrow, too limited, and too inadequate -- how can they give it up without giving up their sense of security and identity?

Only, said this wise observer, when someone lovingly helps them discover a wider, more spacious alternative – a new frame of making sense out of experience.

And I believe, in some ways, that this is just what Jesus was doing. Not only in his teaching, but also in his whole life and ministry. Bringing to us a wider, more spacious alternative to the cramped ways we try to validate our own lives and give them meaning. Helping us realize that the kingdom is nothing we earn by our own moral superiority; but is rather a gift given in the midst of our very human, very real struggles.

It is another kind of righteousness than one of our own making. It is a righteousness which faces the fact that human is human – and that God alone is God.

How can we – who are fallible and finite – ever be righteous in God's sight? How can we who fail in the simplest commandment – you shall not covet … claim to be whole?

Thus, you see, the problem for folk who claim to be righteous, who live by a code (no matter how noble or how high.) There are plenty of examples to those who have tried to do what Jesus ironically states – namely exceed the righteousness of the most pure. Where has it led?

Count Leo Tolstoy, world-famous novelist and Russian landowner, was converted to religion in mid-life and immediately began to take the New Testament literally.

Striving to exceed the righteousness of the scribes and Pharisees, he changed into peasant dress, adopted vegetarianism and total abstinence. He lived the simple life, practiced non-violence and endeavored (without much success) to divide up his vast estates among his serfs. He soon discovered that the step from serfdom to responsible freedom is not short or easy.

Tolstoy persisted in striving to obey every last syllable of the moral law. But, he found that, far from bringing him closer to God; it made him an angry, querulous, tormented old man. He became a sore problem to his wife and children. No longer a great novelist but a tract-writer; not a revealer but a propagandist.

And still (this is Tolstoy's tragedy) he never seemed to have raised the question to which Christ's words point: What is true righteousness?

He failed to see the logic, which Jesus was pressing: That ultimately no one can claim to live with such perfection. And yet, this inward perfection was demanded: Thou shalt not kill. But even anger, even insult, even these inner motives are as serious as the acts, which flow from them. And not just the external deed, but the internal life – the heart – is claimed for righteousness.

Who then can be saved? Who, then, among us is righteous?

No one. At least I hope that there is not one of you who thinks himself or herself righteous – for righteousness is not the human stance: It belongs to God.

There is a wider reality outside the box, which we construct to justify our existence. We can – in freedom – confront the ambiguities of our own human nature; we can let our narrow world-view of self-justification crumble.

For there is One who lovingly – and at great price – lets us see ourselves honestly. Not as those who would be gods, but as humans being. And as human beings who do not live up to our best resolves, who do hurt and destroy one another. Who always carry within us the anxiety of self-concern and self-preservation.

We are the same ones who find in Christ; forgiveness and renewal. The promise of fresh beginnings, and a goodness given, not earned. It is the difference between light and darkness.

Prayer: Dear Lord, be the righteousness of my life. And forgive me for my human nature, which is also a gift from God.

Amen

WINNERS & LOSERS

There is nothing Americans love more, the old saying goes, than a winner! While we may prattle about liking good losers, we really don't make much room for them; either in our affections or on our sports pages.

For many people, winning is everything. Of course, there is winning and there is winning!

The writer of a New Testament letter to the Hebrews 12:1-2 addressed a group of people who could not be called – by any ordinary standard – apparent winners. They were people who lived rather under enormous pressure, threatened daily with defeat.

Since we are surrounded by "so great a cloud of witnesses," the author wrote, "let us lay aside every weight and the sin which doth so easily beset us, and let us run with patience, the race that is set before us.

"Looking unto Jesus the author and finisher of our faith …."

At first glance, the words seem to speak about winning. But notice the qualifications: Since we are surrounded by so great a cloud of witnesses …we are to run the race of life.

Well, just who were those witnesses? None other than people like that old prophet, Jeremiah – who was an apparent failure. A person who got himself literally tossed like rubbish into a pit, despised by his neighbors; because he would not join in the warring, nationalistic theology of his day.

Scarcely – as the world calculates things – a winner.

And who is the model for this race we are to run? Jesus, the pioneer and perfecter of our faith, who ends up disgracefully on a cross – scarcely a winner. Indeed, He reverses the ordinary canons of success and says the last shall be first, and the first last.

Jesus' whole life embodies the reversal of grandiose values. He clearly suggested that there is a kind of winning that comes at too high a price: "For what is a man profited," He cautions in Matthew 16:26, "if he shall gain the whole world, and lose his own soul? ...."

What's it worth to win? What victory is worth your life? Some victories are simply, too costly.

For example, winning at the expense of others costs too much. All of us have, at one time or another, experienced being manipulated by someone else. And we become rightfully leery of the con artist, who wins taking advantage of another person's vulnerability. To operate this way destroys the experience of trust – the basis for relationship.

Or, winning until you have no sympathy for losers is simply winning at too high a price. People who have been both diligent and lucky are particularly prone to think that somehow, they have done it all themselves. And contend that anyone who tries hard enough can be a winner.

Thus, the affluent person may think that no one has to be poor unless he or she chooses to be (ignoring those structures which perpetuate exclusion from opportunity.)

Or the healthy person may think that those who are sick must somehow be responsible for their diseases.

Or the religious person may stand in contempt of another person's lack of faith.

To forfeit any capacity for identification and for caring is simply too high a price to pay for winning. And it is too high a price to pay, when winning becomes one's all-important self-image.

Doris Kearn Goodwin's remarkable biography, *Lyndon Johnson and the American Dream* is basically a sympathetic treatment of this late president. But it demonstrates what could be said of President Johnson and other politicians; who measure their self worth in terms of popularity, their achievements and their victories.

Despair and disillusionment are invited – for whenever such folks lose, their reservoir of ego-strength is diminished. Give him and her enough wins and they can cope. Until the defeats begin to outweigh the sweet victories. When things begin to turn sour; they are left with diminished strength, without inner stamina. For his or her worth as a person has been tied to winning the approval of others.

How many college athletes, for example, have found that life peaked in their early twenties? And somehow, everything since seems downhill. As victories fade; and new heroes arise to replace the old, forgotten ones.

Conversely, there is no virtue in losing for losing's sake. Losing in and of itself can become a destructive affair. Why? Because we all build on strengths – not weaknesses.

God knows that none of us need to deny our weaknesses, our faults, our failures, and our losses. We are finite and fallible folk, insecure even in moments of triumph. We are not angels, but human beings.

Yet, precisely as humans – whatever weakness and sin we have, we also have enormous strength, resiliency, and incredible potential. People, I believe, are often much stronger than we give ourselves credit for. Are able to endure stressful situations and survive. Able to forge new beginnings, when often we have felt unable to take one more step.

We need to encourage one another to resist, then, those attitudes and images, which reinforce the tendency to "bad-mouth" ourselves. If the <u>winner</u> image – ruthlessly adhered to – can be really empty and sad; then equally the <u>victim</u> image can become a propellant for a self-fulfilling prophecy.

For example, my friend Jane sees herself perpetually as a helpless victim – victimized from birth on. Actually, there is some truth in that view of herself. She had been wounded deeply as a youngster, because she hadn't received enough real love and healthy nurturing.

But despite all her vaunted weakness, she has nonetheless managed to extricate herself from some very painful situations. She has, in short, had some successes – even if they have been bracketed by difficulty.

But she still persists in seeing herself as a victim – unable to reach out and affirm herself; say good things about herself, when she has succeeded. She clings somehow to a victim image of herself. Why? Well, who can penetrate the mystery of another person? But it seems that she finds this old image of helplessness familiar and therefore, somehow comfortable and secure.

To see herself in a different, more accurate way as a person able to grow, able to respond to new situations is frightening to her. Hopefully, she will. But it is hard for people to break out of that kind of cycle of self-defeat.

As American writer, Nora Ephron was fond of saying, "Above all, be the heroine of your life, not the victim." And the writer of the letter to the Hebrews instills: Let us run with perseverance the race that is set before us.

How? Well to become winners – but not of the wrong victories acquired at high prices, this is where we need to hear again, the good news of the gospel.

For the central mystery of the gospel is the resurrection of Jesus Christ. He is the Lord of the second chance and the third and the fourth and so on. Life is full of a myriad of possibilities. A mystery which we call grace keeps lighting up our darkness. And illuminates even our failure, at times, with glimpses of insight.

Life isn't won or lost in a single event. No one defeat is all-conclusive. Your life isn't over because all the props have been pulled out from under you, today.

As the orphan Annie sang in the Broadway musical named after her:

> The sun will come out
> Tomorrow
> Bet your bottom dollar
> That tomorrow
> There'll be sun …
> You're always
> A day
> Away!

You still have strengths, which can be tapped. Beyond your own limits, there is a Greater Strength, which can meet you in your weakness and give you new power for the race.

We need to hear that, all of us. We also need to remember that winning and overcoming defeat isn't just a matter of trying harder and harder. It is also, sometimes, a matter of not trying at all. Of stopping, of letting go, of emptying the cup so that God may fill it as He will.

Of pausing long enough to hear that you are special and loved. That you are significant, not because of whatever you've achieved – or failed to achieve. But rather because you <u>are</u>, and because God <u>is</u>. And because God is who He is – and did what He did in Jesus, who came to seek those who are less than whole. Those who know we don't have it all together.

Martin Buber, the profound Jewish philosopher, told the story of a rabbi on his deathbed who laments his life and sees himself as a loser. But he is reminded that in the world to come, he would not be asked why he wasn't Moses. But, why he wasn't himself.

God does not expect you to be someone else – someone with a different history, someone with different patterns of strengths and weaknesses. Rather, He expects us simply to be ourselves and to accept and value ourselves as He accepts and values us.

He loves you even as you are and bids you to run whatever race is set before you. That perseverance comes from a love that accepts you and beckons you to grow toward the full humanity of Jesus Christ.

Prayer: Lord, let me be myself and run my race with all the gifts of strength and kindness and love you have given me.

Amen